Memoirs
of Egotism

BARNES & NOBLE REDISCOVERS

Memoirs of Egotism

Stendhal

Edited by Matthew Josephson

Foreword by Michael Dirda

BARNES & NOBLE

NEW YORK

Barnes & Noble, Inc.
122 Fifth Avenue
New York, NY 10011

ISBN: 978-1-4351-0948-3

Printed and bound in the United States of America

10 9 8 7 6 5 4 3 2 1

Foreword

To the world, Stendhal is the name of one of the world's most eminent novelists, the author of *The Red and the Black* and *The Charterhouse of Parma*. Yet "Stendhal" is only one of many pen-names assumed by Marie-Henri Beyle, just as his two great novels are only a small portion of a sizable and varied literary output. While all serious readers admire the fiction of Stendhal, more than just a Stendhalian "happy few" also love the short, fat, and passionate Beyle, half sentimentalist, half cynical *homme du monde*.

Stendhal—as it's simplest to call him—reveals his truest and most vulnerable self in his correspondence, journals, and such varied works as the treatise *On Love*, the polemical pamphlet (attacking the stultified French drama) *Racine and Shakespeare*, a chatty biography of Rossini (in which the digressions matter more than the narrative), several chronicles of the Parisian art scene, and a travel book called *Walks in Rome*. These, moreover, are just some of his writings published between 1821 and 1830, the time period covered by *Memoirs of Egotism*. This decade also includes Stendhal's first novel *Armance* (about the daring subject of sexual impotence) and closes with his account of the rise and fall of a gifted young man from the provinces, *The Red and the Black*.

Despite all this literary activity, little of it earns a mention in *Memoirs of Egotism*. Stendhal is, in fact, the least self-aggrandizing author one can imagine. He doesn't push his books; he doesn't drop names—indeed, he disguises the identities of many of the people he writes about. During these Paris years, for example, Stendhal spent time with the visiting English essayist William Hazlitt (from whom he may have borrowed the word "egotism"), socialized with the Russian novelist Turgenev, and traveled back to Italy where he stopped off to see his friend the great poet Leopardi. The influential French critic Sainte-Beuve tells us that he attended a dinner party on January 25–26, 1830, where he sat between Victor Hugo and Stendhal. You would think that such luminaries and gatherings might receive a paragraph or two in the *Memoirs of Egotism,* but you would be wrong. At least Stendhal does talk, all too briefly, about his close friend, the short-story writer Prosper Mérimée, author of "Carmen" and "The Venus of Ille."

So what does interest Stendhal? The short answer is his own psychology, the tricks and tics of the memory and the unconscious, his own contradictory nature, equally fascinated with role-playing and sincerity. Scribbled down in 1832, in just under two weeks, these recollections—never completed, like so many of Stendhal's projects—are his first real attempt at autobiography (and would be succeeded by his masterpiece in the genre, *The Life of Henry Brulard,* which treats his childhood and youth). Having lived through the tumultuous Napoleonic era, spent years as a man about town in Milan and Rome, and attempted to make a living as an author during the Bourbon Restoration, the now middle-aged Stendhal suddenly finds himself the French consul in the small Italian town of Civita Vecchia. Bored, he decides "to while away my leisure hours" by recalling his Paris sojourn of the previous decade. He insists that he will scribble as fast as possible—turning out roughly thirty pages per session—and not revise anything, aiming at the kind of authenticity and absolute truth denied more artful and polished pieces of writing.

In fact, the conversational roughness, the constant authorial questioning of motives, the interjection of second thoughts, the sudden shifts and swerves in the narrative, and all the other revelations of a mind actively brooding over its past are what give Stendhal's *Memoirs of Egotism* its magical immediacy. Here is a heart laid bare. The reader, moreover, soon grows as interested in the actual process of revery as in what is being remembered: "Where was I?" Stendhal writes at one point, before adding, "Heavens, how badly written this is!" Elsewhere he notes that "like a respectable woman turned harlot, I must constantly try to overcome the reserve that makes a gentleman reluctant to talk about himself." As always, Stendhal's prose throughout is transparent and unadorned, and every sentence actually says something. "For anyone who has had a taste of the absorbing occupation of writing, there is only a secondary pleasure to be extracted from reading. Often, while at work, I have thought it was only two o'clock when a glance at the clock showed that it was half-past six. This is my only excuse for having blackened so much paper with ink."

At one point Stendhal compares the *Memoirs* to an "examination of conscience," but more accurately it might be called a psychological case-history: This, says Beyle, is how I gradually recovered from my almost suicidal passion for Metilda (an Italian beauty who never even granted him her favors). He does this largely by plunging into a social whirl, made up of now-forgotten cronies, evenings at various salons, and the eventual consolations of new love affairs. To the Parisian society of his time, Stendhal was chiefly known as a witty cynic, with a taste for fashionable clothes. In his own view, he needed his intelligence and wit and splendid dress to compensate for his shortness (he was under five feet, five inches) baldness, obesity, and general lack of good looks. Plus he was now in his late forties, a crisis age for those who, like Stendhal, find that nothing in life matters so much as the promise of happiness in the arms of women. Only the music of Mozart and Cimarosa, the plays of Shakespeare, and the paintings of Tintoretto, he tells us elsewhere, have ever provided him with anything close to the pleasure of falling in love. And as he says here, "it bores me to write of anything but the analysis of the human heart."

So love—lost, sought, or purchased—is a dominant theme throughout the *Memoirs*. Among the book's highlights are Stendhal's chapter about his total fiasco when attempting to enjoy the beautiful courtesan Alexandrine, his portrait of the elderly General Lafayette (who likes to pinch the bottoms of pretty young girls), an idyllic account of "love in a cottage" during a journey to England, and numerous brief anecdotes about the sexual histories and proclivities of the socially prominent:

"Mme. Lavanelle was as dry as a stick, and besides she had no wit, and was incapable of real *passion*; the only thing that could excite her was a glimpse of the handsome thighs of a company of grenadiers in white cashmere breeches as they marched through the Tuileries Gardens."

"One day the eight or ten nieces of Mme. de Montcertin asked her: 'What is love?' To which she replied: 'It is a low, vile thing, of which chambermaids are sometimes accused, and when they are guilty, we send them packing.'"

Besides erotic intrigue, Stendhal is also fascinated, and some-times repulsed, by the political machinations of the toadies and trimmers of the post-Napoleonic world. Yet the creator of the astute Count Mosca in *The Charterhouse of Parma* is certainly not without his own Machiavellian shrewdness. He tells us that "whenever I arrive in a city, I always try to find out: 1) who are the twelve prettiest women; 2) who are the twelve richest men; 3) what man there has the power to have me hanged."

Halfway through these meandering reminiscences—and they are very like a rambling conversation with an imaginary future reader—Stendhal admits: "One can understand every-thing except oneself…" No matter. He also confesses that scribbling away at these pages simply makes him happy—and readers of the *Memoirs of Egotism* will find that its pages will make them happy too.

MICHAEL DIRDA
July 2008

INTRODUCTION

Stendhal as Autobiographer

ALL OF STENDHAL'S LIFE WOULD SEEM TO HAVE BEEN A preparation for the writing of his autobiography. Surely no man brought to such a task more aptitude, more interest, or more passion. His novels themselves, it has often been remarked (like many other great novels) were but concealed autobiographies, or, at any rate, variations upon the theme of his own life. No Jean-Jacques Rousseau, indeed no Marcel Proust ever ransacked his memories more vigorously in search of times past, or interrogated his ego more earnestly, more constantly than he.

Once at a salon in Paris a man, made curious by reports of M. Henri Beyle's somewhat mystifying private character, asked him directly what his business was. The self-styled "Baron de Stendhal" fixed his sharp eye upon his interlocutor and said: "Sir, I am an observer of the human heart." The man, thinking he was a spy of some sort, was frightened and retreated abruptly. But the observation, the analysis of the human heart and its passions had truly been his business in life. And where could one better study this subject than in oneself? Since his boyhood Stendhal had reveled in introspection; he had the faculty of surrendering himself to some emotional experience, then recording it afterward with complete self-consciousness. A great forerunner of modern psychology, he tried to examine himself, and others, with the experimental and dispassionate attitude typified by the new scientists of the time, much as his friend Cuvier, the biologist, dissected animals in his laboratory. Such a method, eschewing all bombast, or sentiment, or self-apology, he believed, had not yet been tried in the medium of literature; certainly not by Rousseau, whose *Confessions* were written in self-defense, nor by Chateaubriand, who had sought to glorify his own character.

Stendhal had a profound sense of history: did he not declare that he had once (toward 1821) postponed committing suicide out of "political curiosity" about what was going to happen next? Born in Grenoble in 1783, in the time of Louis XVI, he was a child of the eighteenth century and also a product of the great French Revolution whose doctrines he ardently embraced. During the span of history that was his lifetime by fifty, surely approaching the most turbulent eras of ancient Rome, he had seen a half dozen dynasties come and go. He had been an officer of Napoleon's army, present at his court and at many of the climactic scenes of the First Empire, including the retreat from Moscow. He had lived through "an ocean of sensations." Indeed he had lived many lives, in different lands, under many different guises: as a soldier, an administrator, a diplomat, a traveler, a gallant, a man of society, and an author. But wherever or whatever he had been, he had never accepted the appearances of things without examination; his had been a detached spirit, ever skeptical, even rebellious at ideas that were à la mode.

He had no religion, no home, no wife. All other obligations had been rejected by him in favor of the perpetual research for personal freedom and self-knowledge. And for those morally conservative times that came after Waterloo, during the Bourbon Restoration in France, this was tantamount to being "a monster of immorality." M. Beyle's books, it was pointed out, were full of scandalous matter and published under a nom de plume. This godless philosopher lived with actresses, and perhaps even took money from them, it was whispered. "The fat Mephistopheles," he was sometimes called.

What few knew was that he was a man of infinite sensibility, for he was noticeably reserved, or in society wore various masks, including that of a wit. His wit concealed a heart that had suffered sorely, a nature that had known great ecstasy and prayer—after its own fashion—not only for women, but for painting, music and literature. In the privacy of his memoirs he would have much to tell us about the real Henri Beyle who had concealed himself from the world.

Like a youth, or rather like a man who continued in the illusion of eternal youth, he was obsessed by the notion that he was misunderstood by his age. (He insisted also that his times were out of touch with realities.) Others, after the restoration of the legitimate monarchy, might turn Royalist in politics, orthodox in religion, or they might "sell out" by merely pretending to be both. He would continue an unbeliever, a liberal, a Jacobin, devoted to the idea of democracy that was now out of favor in Europe. When the Romantic movement in literature (which he had helped to launch) began to embody excesses of style and an intellectual fuzziness that he could not abide, he stood forth as an anti-Romantic, addicted to dryness and factual precision. This was enough to earn him anew the opprobrium of critics who were in fashion. In any case they had long had the habit of slating his books, especially *The Red and the Black,* for alleged bad taste and subversive ideas. His books were little read by the public, and he was being forgotten in his own time—as he was to be forgotten for fifty years after his death. But what of the future?

The future generations, Stendhal guessed shrewdly, would be different. The reader of tomorrow would be republican and equalitarian in his outlook, more concerned with scientific truth than with religious authority. Hence he decided to do what few writers have ever done: to address himself to posterity. Though he was ignored in the 1830s, he predicted: "I shall be read in 1900."

He said to himself cheeringly:

> I can see clearly that many writers who enjoy a great reputation today [1832] are detestable. What would be a blasphemy to say of M. de Chateaubriand now, however, will be a truism in 1880.

This was an apt prophecy, as were so many of his others. The glamorous author of *René* and *Le Génie du Christianisme* was read mainly by schoolboys in the heyday of Zola. Stendhal, on the other hand, was "revived," or rather resuscitated, like Shakespeare, Blake and Herman Melville. He would appear astonishingly "modern" not only in 1890, but in 1950, so that the veriest scraps of his notebooks and letters would be held precious by his devotees of later times.[1]

As an author he had had, in his own time, few friends who approved of his works. The excuse for his memoirs, he tells us, would be that they might be read one day "by some soul like those I admired, such as Mme. Roland, or the mathematician,

Gros." The last named was his inspirational teacher in his boy-hood in Grenoble. The thought of the unborn generations who would read him was almost a fixation. "I regard my works as *lottery tickets,*" he remarks more than once, "and count only on being *reprinted in 1900.*

To the readers of 1900, and after, he would tell some fine truths about his times, as about himself. What a great thing it might be, he exclaims, to have an account of the period written by "a man who was no dupe." He would be unsparing of his contemporaries, as he would be unsparing of himself—this was his justification.

It is therefore a great pity that Stendhal, with such rich equipment for the task, did not live to carry out his grand design of a complete autobiography, perhaps in several large volumes. Two sections of this projected work, fortunately, have been left to us, magnificent fragments of his story, such as none other could have written. They were unearthed among his posthu-mous papers, and published during the Stendhal "revival" that came in France, *circa* 1890, some fifty years after his decease, or almost exactly at the time he had prophesied. The volume of his memoirs called *La Vie d'Henri Brulard,* recording his boyhood and youth, was the first to be published, in 1890; it is already known to English readers. The present work, *Souvenirs d'égotisme,* dealing entirely with his life in Paris from 1821 to 1830, was also found among the Stendhal papers stored in Grenoble, and was published in 1892 by Casimir Striyenski. It is now translated into English for the first time, the transla-tion being based, however, on more recent editions prepared by modern scholars.

Stendhal's *Souvenirs d'égotisme* was actually his first attempt at autobiography, written in 1832, some three years before he returned to an earlier phase of the same subject in the *Henri Brulard*. It was written with much secretiveness; for reasons of discretion the names of friends or acquaintances still living were altered, in some cases. The mystification was further increased when he referred to some of these same characters by their real names in another connection, or bestowed a resounding title on someone of obviously humble origins. He also used his characteristic device of concealing words or ideas that might have compromised him with the police-spies who, he believed, were forever shadowing him—in acrostics made by inverted spelling, or in a none too secret code of foreign terms, English, Italian, etc. *Religion* would be written as *gionreli, prêtres* (priests) as *tréprés,* and *Roi* as K—(after the English word *king*).[2]

The manuscript has the character of a highly private transaction between Stendhal and his unborn public, for he stored it away among his private papers with instructions that it not be published until at least ten years after his death, which came in 1842.

When Stendhal began his *Souvenirs d'égotisme,* the circumstances in which he found himself, serving the French Government again as consul at Civita Vecchia, also made him disposed to write his memoirs without thought of publication save in the distant future. After the Revolution of 1830 had brought the self-declared "liberal" Louis-Philippe, Duke of Orleans, to the throne of France, Stendhal, through the influence of friends at the new court, had at last been given a place in the government service. For more than fifteen years after the downfall of Napoleon there had been no sinecures for him. Like General de Lafayette (of whom he gives such an unconventional portrait in these pages) and other leaders of the anti-

Bourbon party, he had hoped that the Orleans dynasty would be a truly constitutional and democratic monarchy, but soon found himself entirely disillusioned. Yet, as he was "eating off the Budget," he felt that he could not at present publish novels such as *The Red and the Black,* or articles whose tendency would surely irritate a home government showing itself more and more reactionary with every year that passed. His seat was uneasy enough: Metternich's complaints to Paris had driven him from his first assignment at Trieste, in 1831, and at Civita Vecchia he was held in suspicion by the Vatican as a possible Jacobin "conspirator." Now in recent years Henri Beyle, a scion of the *haute bourgeoisie* of Grenoble, had known real poverty: at first during the long period of his voluntary "exile" in Italy, after Waterloo; and then in Paris, where he had returned in 1821 and tried to earn his living by writing, much of it in the nature of pot-boiling.

But as French consul at Civita Vecchia, furnished with some 10,000 francs a year, he could once more live like a gentleman of taste, buying books, objects of art or old furniture, as his heart desired—*provided* that he wrote nothing censurable. This for Stendhal was an impossibility; even in a travel-book, like *Rome, Naples et Florence,* he had shown himself unable to be "right-thinking" or conformist. Therefore, he must write no more. Or if he wrote at all—and to write every day had become a form of relief for him—it must be only privately, for publication at a time when he would no longer be embarrassed by serving the "chief" whom he called "the crookedest of kings." In his notes at this period we find the statement, in English: "*I will print no more.*" He also resolved now to be as discreet as possible in his personal connections. "I have not spoken to any man's sister," he says in a letter to a friend in

Paris. It was a sacrifice that could only have been temporary with him.

He had longed to be in his beloved Italy again, where he had lived the formative years of his youth and learned that the "pursuit of happiness" could be carried on there upon more advantageous terms than in his native France. But the consular post, for all its good pay, proved to be a trap. Instead of living in Milan, the city of his most memorable love adventures, or in Florence, he was imprisoned by his petty consular duties in dreary Civita Vecchia, six hours' carriage-ride from Rome, and many days' journey from Paris.

Formerly he had been the harshest critic of French "vanity" and of the emptiness or superficiality of Parisian society. He had been that rare thing, a Frenchman who in earlier years had preferred Italy, or even, sometimes, England, to France. But in Civita Vecchia the italianate Beyle recognized that the last years in Paris, during the 1820s, had been a period of high interest, even of brilliant achievement so far as the republic of letters was concerned, and perhaps for himself. Only in the salons of Paris, he now said, was there conversation worth the name. And once a week there were the literary dinners at the Café Anglais, where he joined men like Prosper Mérimée, Victor Jaquemorit, the explorer, Sainte-Beuve, Eugène Delacroix, and sometimes the boyish-looking Alfred de Musset. In table talk Stendhal excelled most of his contemporaries, according to Sainte-Beuve.

A quarter of a century of revolution and world war, with its violence and insecurity, is discouraging to artistic production. The stabilized 1820s, however, ushered in a revival of culture: The Romantic School made its belated arrival with the appearance of Lamartine, Hugo, and Alfred de Vigny; Balzac was writing in a garret; and Stendhal himself completed his first novels.

In contrast, Civita Vecchia proved to be a "desert," with no news, no books, no opera, no conversation—nothing, in short, that for Stendhal constituted civilization. And he was beginning to feel his age: it was one of the saddest periods of his life. The writing of his memoirs was undertaken, then, as a form of catharsis. In the silence of his room he talked to himself, unburdened himself without any pretense or affectation. ("Often I lost track of the time: I thought it was two A.M. and saw that it was six-thirty.")

For him it was the time of the crisis of middle-age, sometimes called by the French *"la crise des quarantines,"* but as likely to arrive in the fifties as in the forties. Stendhal, in the summer of 1832, was nearing fifty, more lonely and introspective than ever, in a mood to look back at his own life and take stock.

"What have I been?" he asked himself repeatedly. "Have I made the best use of the circumstances in which chance has placed me?" Had he been a sensible man, a deep man, a fool? Perhaps he had spent too much of his time in "unhappy love affairs," for whose sake he had often sacrificed every worldly advantage. What was the lesson of such a life? *Ecce homo?*

"I ought to write the story of my life, then perhaps I will know what I have been," he observes. His autobiography would be a search for the truth about himself. But this immediately posed the problem of self-interest and indeed of self-love. There would be so many "I's" and "me's" in the book that it would doubtless bore the reader as well as himself. On reading Chateaubriand's *Voyage to Jerusalem* he had noted the wonderful arrogance with which that great man alluded to all that

he had been and done. "I have never seen such stinking egotism in anyone," Stendhal noted at the time. What, then, would
be the justification for his own variety of self-interest? How
could his own memoirs avoid becoming a work of "abominable egotism?"

Well, he for his part would approach the problem quite dif-
ferently from Chateaubriand. The study of the human heart was
a worthwhile venture in itself; it was becoming virtually a science. (The word "psychology" was not yet much in usage then
in the sense in which we now understand it.) Our knowledge of
such matters, he declared, had made giant strides since the days
of the admirable Montesquieu a century earlier, and Stendhal
felt that he had much that was new to reveal. He would apply
himself to the study of his own case "without sparing this animal," as he said. He would expose all his own weaknesses and
errors. Thus his would be an "egotism that was sincere"; that
is, it would represent a new way of picturing human emotions.
Hence the title he chose for his autobiography was *Souvenirs
d'égotisme*, literally "Memoirs of Egotism." The word "egotism," however, a new word in French, was not at all intended
in the pejorative sense, denoting a narrow self-interest, which it
now has, but rather to define the process of concentrated self-
examination which Stendhal proposed to carry out.

To his admirers of later generations, to men like Taine
and Nietzsche, Stendhal possessed the psychologist's eye to
a remarkable degree; he had the faculty of recording all the
inward, unexpressed emotions that accompanied an experience. For instance, in the account here of his meeting with a
man he profoundly admired, the philosopher Destutt de Tracy,
he remembers not only what he said, but that which he had
felt and left unsaid: his embarrassment in the presence of the

great man, his exaggerated gratitude, his awkwardness, his incoherence. He was aware of the "irrational" or unconscious elements of the mind long before the later nineteenth century psychologists and the men of the Freudian school arrived on the scene. And nowhere in his writings is this faculty of psychological observation more marked than in his autobiographical pieces. In the study of his childhood, which he wrote somewhat later (*Henri Brulard*) appeared certainly one of the first clinical observations of the Oedipus Complex, based on his own relations with his parents.

In addition, he shows himself in his memoirs as one of the most painstaking of witnesses. Frequently he pauses to differentiate between that which he himself remembers, by naming the time and the place, and that which may have come to him by hearsay. He girds himself also to recount the most painful or humiliating experiences that have befallen him, without glossing them over. "Will I have the courage to tell the truth?" he exclaims more than once. The theme of his adventures in love was to have loomed large in his memoirs. However, he begins his account not with some easy triumph, but with a fiasco, an unaccountable failure of nerve in the arms of a handsome courtesan. Such honesty cost him clearly, both in the pleasantries of his friends and the misrepresentations of later commentators. There was quite evidently nothing wrong with him—judging from the letters of Mme. de Curial—beyond an occasional attack of overwrought nerves.

He used various special devices to achieve the highest degree of objectiveness and accuracy, by his own standards. It was not the *mot juste*, but the exact communication of thought that he desired; hence he schooled himself to set forth his observations as soberly as possible, as though he were a botanist studying curious plants. To be "literary," or to indulge in bombast, was to *lie*. On the other hand, the unfeigned candor, the simplicity with which he describes some deep-felt emotion, as in parting from a woman he loved, have an effect that is all the more convincing.

He must write his memoirs like letters to an intimate friend, he tells himself. The test is to be whether he is enjoying the process; on one night it may seem boring to him, on another: "I have enjoyed writing this . . ." he remarks at the end of the session. Plainly enough he gropes toward that confessional therapy that was to be used by psychiatrists so extensively a hundred years after his time.

Finally, he strove for speed, for a sort of *automatic* writing of the impressions that crowded into his mind, whether they seemed connected or disassociated. Thus he hoped to come "close to Nature" in her most unforeseen (*imprévu*) or unconscious aspects. In these memoirs there are moments when he floats on the stream of consciousness, apparently at random. He would sit down for three hours or so and write some twenty pages of manuscript, three or four thousand or more words at a session—for he was a rapid worker—without stopping for an instant to correct, to alter, or to arrange his thoughts. On one occasion, after having worked in this manner, he concluded with the remark: "Written without revision *in order not to lie.*"

With a form of attack so novel, it is not surprising that Stendhal, as the late Paul Valéry said, achieved the most individual tone of his age. It is always that of informal conversation, for he wore his curious erudition lightly. One must grow accustomed to the rapid, sometimes elliptical character of his thought, to his oddities of reservation and punctilio, his precise way of measuring feelings or experiences, his fetish for "logic" above all; then the intellectual humor, the freshness of his discourse grows upon one, much as his dinner talk and his "improvisations" used to entertain his contemporaries. For he constantly warns himself that he must be interesting or amusing to his future readers; no writing was worth the paper it was written on, in his belief, unless its author had some ideas to communicate. The *Souvenirs*, brief and incomplete though they are, are full of authentically Stendhalian reflections on the art of life, letters, politics, love and even crime. Although he himself was law-abiding, Stendhal greatly enjoyed accounts of crimes, not of the habitual or mercenary variety, but *unpremeditated*, that is, deriving from "unexpected" or unconscious motives.

The reader must recall that before Stendhal, as for a considerable period after him, the novel was not distinguished for its psychological finesse. The characters presented by Fielding and Richardson, even by Rousseau and Benjamin Constant in their autobiography-novels, had relatively simple appetites and reactions. (Stendhal considered all of these recent writers far beneath Shakespeare in discernment of the range of human motives.) But in Stendhal's memoirs, as in his novels, you have the portraits of complex, nervous characters, embodying deep contradictions or ambivalence of motives. And of these none is more complex and contradictory than the observer of the human heart himself.

In the opening pages of the *Souvenirs* he wishes to convey something of the boundless grief he feels at having been rejected by Metilda Viscontini of Milan after three years of courtship. He does not attempt any tragic tirades, but relates simply that he considered suicide, by falling off a horse while climbing the Alps. Yet he only succeeded in making himself ridiculous, for the guide accompanying him told him unfeelingly that his death would be bad for business. He wants to die, but at the same time remarks jestingly that he is "afraid he might hurt himself," though he is known for his hardiness and physical courage. His plans to kill himself went no further than *drawing a picture of a pistol* on the pages of letters or manuscripts.

The stunning effect of an immense grief shows itself not in loud lamentations, but in a mood of torpor. But he is also a man of pride. He desires to shun his friends on returning to Paris, yet on the other hand fears terribly that they may *divine* his state of melancholy and its cause. That he should be weeping over a woman whom he "had never had" would seem to them the height of the ridiculous. And in France, he points out, all men are ruled by their fear of appearing ridiculous. Therefore he plays the gay dog with more abandon than ever; to hide his sorrow he becomes a madcap; he runs off with his old bachelor cronies to a bordello. You do not find such human complexity, at once diverting and disturbing, in Balzac, or even in Flaubert or Zola, in fact, not until the appearance of the great Russian novelists, Dostoevski, and Tolstoy, who studied the forgotten Stendhal with profit.

These memoirs then take up his life at the time of his reluctant return to Paris in 1821, after seven years of happy "exile" in Milan. He had just suffered his greatest "defeat," the final rejection of his proposals by Metilda, who was to his mind the noblest woman he had ever met. Life in Milan had become inconvenient for other reasons as well: because of his friendly connections with the Italian *Carbonari* who were plotting against the Austrian rulers of Italy, M. Beyle had been invited by the police to leave the city.

To clarify some of Stendhal's mystifying allusions to persons and incidents not fully described in his *Souvenirs,* unfinished as they are, perhaps some added details about his life at this period need to be introduced here. In Paris in 1821 his heart to be sure is all in splinters; he is reading proofs of his treatise *On Love,* which is a tribute to his long passion for Metilda; but he also renews a few of his old, pre-Waterloo friendships and prepares to enter into the controversy between the Classicists and the Romanticists with his pamphlet "Racine and Shakespeare," which contributes to his reputation among the people of the salons. After several years of brooding over his lost love—Metilda was fated to die young of a sudden illness—he seems at last willing and ready to be "cured." The agency of recovery appears in the person of the Countess Clémentine de Curial, a handsome woman of about thirty-five, with fine eyes and an aquiline nose. She is the daughter of his patroness of Napoleonic days, the Countess Beugnot, and Beyle had known her since her girlhood. When they meet again she is married, but very unhappy because of her husband's brutalities to her, and her eyes often rest affectionately upon the amusing Beyle. In one of the passages of the *Souvenirs* we recognize as referring to Clémentine, her mother twits her about this.

Though Beyle's observations upon his private conduct and his frailties are often brutally frank, he shows a gentlemanly reserve in approaching the subject of the women he greatly loved. It must be remembered that the Countess de Curial was still living when he wrote this memoir. She was moreover a well-known social figure in Paris and at the court, and he feared that some intruder (the secret police?) might pry into his papers. Her story was to have been the dominant theme of these recollections of the 1820s in Paris; yet Beyle can scarcely bring himself to speak of her openly before his narrative breaks off, during the burning days of summer at Civita Vecchia. Nor did he revert to the subject before his death in 1842, though her letters, with his explanatory remarks in the margins, were carefully preserved among his private papers.

To clear up the confusion deliberately introduced by Stendhal's references to this person under different names and unlikely connections, it should be said that he needed little more encouragement than her friendly glances to come to the point of offering her consolation for her unhappy marriage. On May 22, 1824, his proposals were accepted, and with delight he records himself as "cured," cured, that is, of his passion for Metilda. But after a liaison lasting two years, rather long for Stendhal, we find that his battered old heart is smashed to pieces again.

The high-spirited Clémentine, whom her lover described as the most intelligent of his women friends, understood Beyle well, and yet their secret attachment was marked by repeated quarrels and storms. "Your love is the most fearful misfortune that may befall a woman," she charged in one of her letters, adding that he had robbed her of health and happiness, and had tortured her with his famous "system" of love, as developed in his treatise on that subject. "And yet I love you, I love you, I still love you," she closed. It was for Clémentine that Stendhal hid for three days in a cellar at her chateau in the country—when her husband suddenly arrived—while she stealthily brought him food and wine at night and attended to all his wants herself. It was for her he once prepared to fight a duel with a presumed rival—said to have been General de Caulaincourt—a meeting that fortunately never came off, for it would have caused scandal ruinous to a woman in Clémentine's position.

Following one of their recurrent lovers' quarrels in 1826, Stendhal suddenly ran off to England (a trip whose details he sometimes confuses in the *Souvenirs* with an earlier one, in 1821) under the impression that Clémentine was deceiving him. Whether this was true or false, she now determined that he was not to return to her and be forgiven as usual. This break, he noted in his quaint English, was *"the most sensitive misfortune of his life."* Ten years later Prosper Mérimée saw him in tears because Clémentine still would not take him back. She was then forty-eight, and he well on in his sixth decade, but to him she was eternally young. At the age of fifty the Countess de Curial, deserted by her latest lover, and embittered at the thought of growing old, committed suicide. There is reason to believe that Clémentine inspired the remarkable portrait in the second volume of *The Red and the Black* of Mathilde de la Mole, the rebellious daughter of a Royalist minister who threw herself at the head of Julien Sorel.

In his memoirs, however, Stendhal shields the Countess de Curial by giving her three different aliases: "Mme. Doligny," "Countess Dulong," and "Fanny Berthois." Her mother he calls "Countess Doligny," and also, either by design or forgetfulness, by her true name, Countess Beugnot. The names of his personal friends are also disguised: Prosper Mérimée, whose first published work was *Le Théatre de Clara Gazul,* appears under the rather transparent nom de guerre of "Count Gazul." Mérimée was the only writer among his contemporaries in France whom Stendhal approved of, particularly for his dry, clear style and artistic restraint. In his youth the author of *Carmen* was heavily indebted to his older friend and mentor, who, to be sure, leaves us a portrait of Mérimée touched with a bit of acid. But Mérimée, after Stendhal's death, wrote of him with far greater cruelty.

Among the other friends in the bachelor circle described in the *Souvenirs*, there is Baron Adolphe de Mareste, here called "Lussinge," who was known as a man of taste and wit, and also as the disciple of the "fat Mephistopheles," Beyle. Mareste was for many years the administrative chief of the Prefecture of Police in Paris. Through him and through Joseph Lingay, described under the pseudonym of "Maisonnette," who was a ghostwriter for one Prime Minister after another, Stendhal had access to all the backstage gossip of the Bourbon and Orleans dynasties. Somewhat confusing is his use of the alias "Barot" for his Gargantuan friend Lolot, the businessman who usually organized their revels. For at the period there existed a real Barot, Odilon Barot, whom Stendhal also mentions, and who later became a cabinet minister under Louis-Philippe. These and other disguised names, where it has been possible to trace them, have been indicated in footnotes accompanying the text.

Aside from their very particular literary qualities these *Souvenirs* form a unique historical document of the social life in Paris not only in the 1820s, but also, through some lengthy digressions, of the Napoleonic era, when the young Henri Beyle held the sinecure of Inspector of the Imperial Furnishings. He was an inveterate theatre-goer, and students of the history of the theatre will enjoy his precise account of the most celebrated French actor of the age, Talma, who was Napoleon's favorite. Also that of the great prima donna Mme. Pasta, internationally famous for her part in spreading the taste for Italian opera to France, England, and indeed all over Europe. Now Giuditta Pasta was for years Stendhal's good friend. But being a professional actress, for all her world fame and wealth she could not appear at the salons of conservative Restoration society. Hence Stendhal, after making his round of visits to the respectable salons he frequented, late at night, toward twelve, always repaired to Mme. Pasta's for a game of cards in an Italian circle that brought back to him cherished memories of Milan. This habit gave rise to some sly talk that mortified him deeply, and which he took pains, in these memoirs, to denounce.

Yet he himself, like many other gifted writers and moralists, was an impassioned gossip, and he patently shows an all-too-human pleasure in setting down "little true facts" about the great persons or the stuffed shirts he met, especially if they were aristocrats.

The figure that M. Beyle presented to his contemporaries in the 1820s and 1830s must have been oddly at variance with the morbidly sensitive "youth" of the self-portrait in these memoirs. To offset his "head of an Italian butcher" and his short, stout body, he wore a wig, dyed his whiskers, and dressed always in the height of fashion, often in a coat of a bronze shade with cream-colored trousers and waistcoat and the richest of cravats. A stovepipe or fine beaver tilted upon his head, a cigar and a cane, completed the bizarre picture.

"Tuesday at Mme. Ancelot's, Wednesday at M. Gérard's, Saturday at M. Cuvier's, and three suppers a week at the Café Anglais, and I am in touch with everything going on in Paris!" he remarks. Mme. Ancelot was the rich wife of a poet and Academician, whose salon all of literary Paris frequented; Baron Gérard was the most highly paid and one of the worst portrait painters of the time; and Cuvier, the friend of Ampère, was one of the leading scientists. In addition, Stendhal went regularly on Sundays to the home of Count de Tracy, a fine specimen of the old noblesse, who had also been the friend of Thomas Jefferson and a powerful supporter of the French Republic. The Tracy

salon was one of the chief gathering places of the Liberal oppo-
sition leaders, and General de Lafayette was of course its lion.
At this period Stendhal did much anonymous hack-writing to
supplement his tiny private income, and depended upon his
social connections for news of books, music, or art-salons to
be reviewed.

You see him teasing and provoking people as he moves about.
At the Tracys' he makes proposals for the liquidation of the ultra-
Royalists and the nobility, proposals so cruel that the genteel liberals present are deeply shocked. At the literary salons he mocks
Chateaubriand as "the Grand Lama," the distinguished Victor
Cousin as "humbug that takes itself seriously," and Lamartine as
a little "Byron in French paint." At Mme. Ancelot's he appears
one day in disguise, pretending to be a fat merchant who provi-
sions the French army with stockings and underwear. Literature
and art, he warns the company present in a mad tirade, are
dreamy and useless things; the great future is for those who make
woolen nightcaps or stockings! But besides playing the wit he
could be courageous too, as when he told his hearers that "only
the lower orders of people possess energy"; or when he ridiculed
contemporary writers for their conformity and right-thinking,
saying: "When it comes to base conduct, one should leave that
to the Prime Minister." At another salon you see him disputing so
vehemently with the romantic historian Augustin Thierry that he
leaves the house, never to return. But everywhere he sings for his
supper, or as he phrased it, "paid for his ticket of admission," by
helping to drive away boredom. "He used to conceal his sadder
feelings under cover of his jests," wrote Mme. Virginia Ancelot in
her *Salons de Paris*. And another admiring hostess of the period
said discerningly that the "fat Mephistopheles" was "really an
angel who pretended to be a demon."

At any rate he is *himself* in these brief, crowded *Souvenirs,* bubbling with wit or malicious fun at night, but showing his acquaintances a face of stone when he takes his morning walk in the streets of Paris, his thoughts concentrated on his books, his memories, or his unrequited loves.

These memoirs were written in haste, to distract his own mind; they remained unrevised. But Stendhal indicates here his desire that they be published, if at all, in the spontaneous form they originally assumed. Defects of style they have indeed, yet they possess the rare, the inestimable merit of helping us to know Stendhal.

MATTHEW JOSEPHSON

CHAPTER I[*]

ROME, JUNE 20, 1832.

TO WHILE AWAY MY LEISURE HOURS IN THIS FOREIGN LAND, I have thought of writing a short memoir of my experiences during my last sojourn in Paris, from June 21, 1821, to November . . . , 1830, a period of nine and a half years. For two months, ever since the novelty of my position here has worn off, I have been prodding myself to undertake some project or other. Without work, the vessel of life has no ballast.

I confess that I should lack the courage to write if not for the belief that some day these pages would appear in print and would be read by someone I admired, such as Mme. Roland or M. Gros, the mathematician.[1]

Did I make the most of my chances for happiness during the nine years I have just spent in Paris? What kind of man am I? Am I a man of good sense? A man of good sense with some depth?

---

[*] Not to be printed until ten years after my death, out of consideration for the persons named. However, two-thirds of them are dead as of today.—*Beyle.*

Have I a remarkable mind? To tell the truth, I do not know. Moreover I rarely ponder over these basic questions because I live for the moment, and besides my judgments vary with my moods. My judgments are no more than fleeting impressions.

As I begin this self-examination, pen in hand, let us see whether I shall arrive at something *positive,* something that will remain *true for a long time* in my own eyes. How shall I react to what I am writing about now when rereading it, say, in 1835, if I live till then? Will it be the same as in the case of my printed works? A deep feeling of melancholy comes over me whenever, for want of other books, I read my own again.

For the last month, since I have given the subject some thought, I have felt a genuine reluctance to write only in order to talk about myself, or of the number of my shirts, or of my wounded pride. On the other hand, I am far from France, and I have read all the amusing books that have reached this country. At heart I should have preferred to write a book of imagination, based on a love affair that took place in Dresden in August 1813, in the house next door to the one in which I was living, but the humdrum duties of my office break in upon me rather frequently; or, to put it better, when taking up my pen I can never be sure of an hour without interruptions. Petty annoyances of this sort discourage the imaginative faculty, and when I return to my tale, I find my earlier thoughts tasteless. To which a wise man will answer that one must master oneself. But I reply: It is too late, I am 49 years old. After so many adventures it is high time for me to think of ending my days in as unobjectionable a manner as possible.

My principal objection to writing the story of my life was not the vanity that it required. A book on such a subject is like any other; it is quickly forgotten if it is dull. But I dreaded spoiling the happy moments I had known by describing them, by dissecting them. Now that is precisely what I shall not do; I shall leave out happiness altogether.

The genius of poetry is dead, but the demon of *suspicion* is come into the world. I am firmly convinced that the only antidote for this, the only thing that might make the reader forget the eternal *I* of the author, is complete sincerity.

Shall I have the courage to tell of humiliating incidents without extenuating them by lengthy apologies? I hope so.

Although my ambitions have miscarried, I do not believe that men are evil, nor do I consider myself to have been persecuted by them. I regard them as automatons driven by *vanity* in France, and elsewhere by all the passions, vanity included.

I do not really know myself, after all, and it is this that sometimes saddens me in the middle of the night, when I brood over it. Am I good, bad, intelligent, stupid? Was I wise enough to take advantage of the opportunities presented to me by the absolute power of Napoleon (whom I always adored) in 1810, or by our downfall in 1814, or by our later efforts to pull ourselves out of the mire in 1830? I fear not; I acted according to my mood of the moment, in a haphazard way. If another man had asked my advice about a similar situation, I might have given him counsel of great value. Friends who were my intellectual rivals have often complimented me on this talent.

In 1814 Count Beugnot, then prefect of police, offered me the post of commissary of the city of Paris.[2]

I was in an admirable position to accept, since I had not solicited any office, and yet I answered in such a way as not to give him any encouragement. To M. Beugnot, a man with vanity enough for two Frenchmen, this must have come as a great shock. The man who took the post retired after four or five years, weary of making money hand over fist, which, it is said, he managed to do without stealing. The supreme contempt I felt for the Bourbons—whom I then considered foul scum— made me quit Paris a few days after turning down M. Beugnot's obliging offer. My heart, torn by the triumph of all I despised and could not hate, was comforted only by the faint stirrings of love that I was beginning to feel for Countess Dulong, whom I saw every day at the home of M. Beugnot, and who ten years later was to play a great part in my life.[3]

At that time she singled me out, not as a likable man, but as a strange one. She looked on me as the friend of a woman who was extremely ugly but of a noble character, Countess Beugnot. I have always reproached myself for not having been in love with Mme. Beugnot. What a pleasure it would have been to exchange confidences with a woman of such comprehension!

For the last three pages I have felt that this preface is too long, but I must begin with a subject so sad and so painful to me that even now my spirits flag, and I am half-inclined to drop the pen. But at the first moment of solitude I should regret it.

I left Milan for Paris on the . . . of June, 1821, with a sum of 3,500 francs, as I remember, convinced that the only pleasure I could look forward to was to blow out my brains when that money was spent. After three years of intimacy, I was parting from a woman I adored, a woman who loved me in return, but had never given herself to me.

Even after the passage of so many years, I am still at a loss to unravel the motives for her conduct. She was in deep disgrace in Milan, although she had never had but one lover; this was how the women of good society there avenged themselves for her superior qualities. Poor Metilda never knew how to outwit or disconcert her enemies.[4]

Some day, perhaps when I am very old and desiccated, I may have the courage to write of the years 1818, 1819, 1820 and 1821.

In 1821 it was only with the greatest difficulty that I resisted the temptation to shoot myself. I used to draw the picture of a pistol in the margin of a paltry love-story I was scribbling at the time (it was when I was living in the Acerbi house). It seems to me that what prevented me from ending it all was my curiosity in political matters. Perhaps too, without my suspecting it, I had some fear of hurting myself.

At last I took leave of Metilda.

"When will you return?" she asked.

"Never, I hope."

There followed a last hour of tergiversation and fruitless talk; a single word of hers might have changed the course of my life, but alas, not for very long. That angelic soul, contained in so fair a body, left this world in 1825.

At length, on the . . . of June, I departed, in what state of mind can well be imagined. I journeyed from Milan to Como, at every step fearing, nay believing, that I would be obliged to turn back.

I felt that I could not remain in Milan without dying, and yet I could not leave it without feeling my heart torn from me. It seemed as if I were leaving my life behind me, but what am I saying? what was life compared to her? I expired with every step I took that led away from her. Like Shelley, I breathed only in sighs.[5]

I was in a sort of stupor, conversing with the postilions and giving sober answers to their comments on the price of wine, weighing all the factors that might make it go up or down a penny. What was most fearful for me was to look into my own mind. The road led through Airolo, Bellinzona, Lugano (these names make me shudder even today—June 20, 1832).

When I reached Saint-Gothard, then an abominable place (similar to the Cumberland Mountains in the north of England, except that there were precipices here) I insisted on riding through the pass on horseback, with some little hope that I might fall and be flayed alive, by way of distraction. Although I was once a cavalry officer, and have spent my life falling from horses, in reality I am terribly afraid of having my mount slip on loose stones and crush me beneath his hooves.

The courier who accompanied me at last stopped me and said that he was not greatly concerned for my life, but that if I were killed it would reduce his profit, as no one would ever want to come with him over the mountains when it became known that one of his travelers had fallen into the abyss.

"What! Haven't you guessed that I have the pox?" I said. "I am unable to go on foot."

At last we reached Altdorf, the courier cursing his lot all the way. I gazed at everything about me as if in a trance. I am a great admirer of William Tell, although according to the official version in all countries, no such man ever existed. At Altdorf, as I remember, I was much moved on seeing a bad statue of William Tell in a stone smock, all the more touching for the very reason that it was so bad.

There now, I said to myself, lapsing into a mood of gentle melancholy that for the first time supplanted my hopeless grief, there one sees what becomes of the most beautiful things in the eyes of vulgar people. Such art thou, Metilda, in Mme. Traversi's drawing-room![6]

The sight of this statue softened me a little. I inquired about the location of Tell's chapel.

"You will see it tomorrow," I was told.

But the next day I set off on my travels again in very bad company, that of some Swiss officers attached to the guard of Louis XVIII, who were returning to Paris.*

I have never cared for France, particularly the region around Paris, which proves that I am a bad Frenchman and a wicked man, as Mlle. Sophie . . . the stepdaughter of M. Cuvier, told me later.[7]

I was therefore in extremely low spirits as I traveled from Basle to Belfort, leaving the high if not beautiful mountains of Switzerland for the flat and dreary Champagne country.

The women are ungainly, to be sure, in the village of . . . , where I saw them in their wooden shoes and coarse blue stockings. But later I was struck by the politeness, the affability and precision of their rustic speech.

Langres has the same situation as Volterra, a city I adored at that time because it had been the theatre of one of the most daring exploits in my war against Metilda.[8]

In Langres I was reminded of Diderot, who, as everyone knows, was the son of a cutler of that town. I thought of his *Jacques le Fataliste,* the only one of his works that I admire. I rate it much more highly than his *Voyage d'Anacharsis,* the *Traité des études,* and a hundred other books esteemed by the pedants.

The worst misfortune that could befall me, I exclaimed to myself, would be that my friends in Paris, those cold-blooded men amongst whom I was going to live, should learn of my passion for a woman I had not even possessed!

---

* Here four pages describing the trip from Altdorf to Gersau, Lucerne, Basle, Belfort, Langres, Paris. Concerned as I am with moral problems, physical description bores me. In the last two years I have not written a dozen pages of that sort of thing.—*Beyle.*

I said this to myself in June 1821, and I see now, in June 1832, for the first time, while writing these words, that this fear recurred again and again, and was in fact the dominant motive of my life for ten years. It was because of this that I came *to have wit,* something that I used to scorn utterly in Milan in 1818 when I was madly in love with Metilda.

I arrived in Paris, which I found worse than ugly, in fact insulting in my unhappy mood, with that one idea: *not to be found out.*

At the end of a week, seeing that political activity was at a stand still, I decided to profit by my suffering to t L 18.[9]

Thereupon I lived somehow for several months of which I can remember nothing. In order to obtain some word of Metilda indirectly, I overwhelmed my friends in Milan with letters, but those who disapproved of my folly never mentioned her name to me when they replied.

In Paris I took lodgings at No. 47 rue de Richelieu, in the Hotel de Bruxelles, kept by a M. Petit, former valet de chambre of one of the Damas brothers. The civility, the grace, the punctilio of M. Petit, his complete lack of sentimentality, his aversion to any display of excessive feeling, his keen recollection of the triumphs of vanity thirty years earlier, his scrupulous honesty in money matters, all made him in my eyes the perfect model of the Frenchman of the old regime. I hastened to entrust him with the 3,000 francs still left to me, and against my will he handed me a scrap of a receipt that I promptly lost. This circumstance annoyed him considerably several weeks or months later when I asked for my money back in order to go to England, driven there by the mortal loathing I felt for everything in Paris.

I have very few recollections of that time of storm. Objects slipped past me without catching my eye, or were disregarded even if they came within range of my vision. My thoughts were on the Piazza Belgiojoso in Milan. I must pull myself together now and try to remember the homes in Paris at which I used to call regularly.

Chapter II

Here is the portrait of a man of parts with whom I used to spend all my mornings for eight years. There was some esteem in my feeling for him, but no friendship.

I had put up at the Hotel de Bruxelles because a certain Piedmontese was stopping there, the coldest, most inflexible man I ever knew, an exact counterpart of Rancor (in the *Roman Comique*). This man, the Baron Lussinge, was thirty-six in 1821, having been born around 1785. From 1821 to 1831 he was my boon companion, and he only began to stand aloof and be somewhat uncivil to me when I acquired the reputation of a man of wit, after the dreadful misfortune that befell me on September 15, 1826.[1]

Short and thickset, of stocky figure, so nearsighted that he was unable to see anything at three paces, M. de Lussinge always dressed shabbily to save money, which was such an obsession with him that he used to pass the time during our morning walks by drawing up all kinds of budgets for the personal expenditures of a bachelor living alone in Paris. Yet he was a man of rare sagacity. With my fine romantic illusions I was inclined to rate the genius, virtue, fame and happiness of a man passing in the street as worth, let us say, thirty points, when fifteen would have been more accurate; he on the other hand would count them as worth only six or seven.

This was the main subject of our conversation for eight years, and yet we sought each other out from one end of Paris to the other.

Though he was then only thirty-six or -seven, Lussinge had the head and heart of a man of fifty-five. He was only deeply moved by events that concerned him personally; then he would go quite mad, as at the time of his marriage. Aside from that, he always found a target for his irony in any display of emotion. Lussinge had, in fact, only one religion: a reverence for high birth. He himself stems from a family that held high rank in le Bugey in 1500; his ancestors followed the Dukes of Savoy to Turin when they became the royal house of Sardinia.

Lussinge had been educated in Turin at the same academy as Alfieri; there he had acquired the profound malice so characteristic of the Piedmontese, a trait in which they are supreme, but which is in reality nothing more than a deep mistrust of men and destiny. I find more than one sign of this in Rome, but among the Romans there are warm passions as well, and as the theatre is larger, one finds less middle-class pettiness.

JUNE 21.

Nonetheless I was fond of Lussinge until he grew rich, then progressively avaricious, timid, and at length, toward January 1830, disagreeable in his relations with me, in fact, almost dishonest.

He had a mother who was very parsimonious but even more foolish, and was capable of giving away all her property to the priests. Lussinge decided to marry, as a way of tying up his mother's property legally and preventing her from handing it all over to her confessor. His intrigues, his deportment when pursuing a woman used to afford me much amusement. Once he was on the point of asking for the hand of a charming girl who would have made him happy, besides perpetuating our friendship. I am referring to the daughter of General Gilly, now Mme. Douin, the wife of a solicitor, I believe. But as the general had been condemned to death after 1815, such a connection would have horrified the noble baroness, my friend's mother. Then by a great stroke of luck he just missed tying himself up with an arrant coquette, now Mme. Varambon. In the end he married a perfect ninny, a tall girl who would have been handsome if she had had a nose. The father-confessor of this silly young woman was Mgr. de Quélen, the archbishop of Paris, whose drawing room she used as her confessional. By chance I had learned some details of the love-affairs of this archbishop, who perhaps at that very time had as his mistress Mme. de Podinas, lady-in-waiting to the Duchess de Berry. Mme. de Podinas, some time before this, or maybe later, had also been the mistress of the renowned Duke de Ragusa. One day I was indiscreet enough—that is one of my numerous faults, if I am not mistaken—to tease Mme. de Lussinge a bit about the archbishop.

We were at the home of the Countess d'Avelles.[2]

"Cousin," she cried furiously, "tell M. Beyle to hold his tongue!"

From that moment on she was my enemy, although occasionally she would relapse, oddly enough, into coquetry. But I see I am embarked on a very long episode; I will go on with it, however, for after all I used to see Lussinge twice a day for eight years. Later I will return to that huge and buxom baroness, his wife, who is nearly five feet six inches tall.[3]

With her dowry, added to his salary as chief clerk at the Prefecture of Police, and an allowance from his mother, Lussinge by 1828 had in all an income of twenty-two or twenty-three thousand francs a year. From that moment on he was obsessed by one idea: the fear of losing his money. Though he despised the Bourbons—not as much as I, who have some political integrity, but despising them nevertheless as maladroit—he finally reached a point where he could no longer bear to hear of their blunders without falling into a towering rage. (He was quick to sense any threat to his property, from whatever direction.) Every day there was some fresh item of news to worry him, as can be seen from the papers between 1826 and 1830. Lussinge used to spend his evenings at the theatre, never in society, as I did, for he was somewhat ashamed of his position.[4]

In the morning when we met at the café for breakfast I would therefore tell him any news I had learned the preceding evening. As a rule we used to joke about our political differences, but on January 3, 1830, as I remember, he flatly denied some fact or other reflecting on the Bourbons that I had heard at the home of M. Cuvier, then councilor of state, and a strong supporter of the government. This blunder on Lussinge's part was followed by a prolonged silence; we passed the Louvre without speaking. At that time I had only what was strictly necessary to live on, while he, as I have pointed out, had an income of twenty-two thousand francs. For a year I had suspected him of trying to assume an attitude of superiority towards me. In our political discussions, for example, he would say:

"But as for you, you have no fortune at stake."

At any rate I came to a most painful decision; I resolved to change my café without telling him. For nine years I had been going to the Café de Rouen every day at half-past ten in the morning. The place was kept by M. Pique, a reputable citizen, and Mme. Pique, then a good-looking woman, whom our mutual friend Maisonnette used to pay five hundred francs each time she granted him her favors.[5]

After my rift with Lussinge I retreated to the Café Lemblin, the well-known Liberal café, also situated in the Palais-Royal. Thereafter I met Lussinge only once in two weeks. Later on we made efforts from time to time to renew our intimacy, which had become a necessity for both of us, but there was never enough drive behind it to be successful. On several occasions afterwards we found neutral territory in music or painting, on which he was well informed, but the moment we approached the subject of politics and he began to tremble for his 22,000 francs, all his churlishness would come to the fore again. There was no way of carrying on. His hard common sense, I must admit, checked my tendency to lose myself in my poetic illusions. On the other hand, my lively spirits—for I grew lively or rather learned the art of appearing so—distracted him from his somber and malicious humors, and even from the terrible *fear of losing his money*.

When I found a modest post in 1830, I have reason to believe that Lussinge considered the salary too high for my qualifications. But at any rate, from 1821 to 1828 I used to meet him twice daily and except for the subject of love and my literary projects, of which he had no understanding, we babbled on at great length about every one of my actions as we walked in the Tuileries gardens and along the Quai du Louvre, on the way to his office. Between eleven and twelve o'clock we were always together, and very often he succeeded in distracting my mind from the gnawing grief of which he knew nothing.

Now at last I have come to the end of this long episode, but after all it concerned the chief personage of these recollections.

Later, to my great amusement, I inoculated him with my fren-
zied passion for Mme. Azur, whose faithful lover he has been
these last two years. And what is more amusing still, he has
rendered her faithful to him.[6]

I must say that she is one of the least *puppet-like* French-
women I have ever met.

But let us not get ahead of our story. In telling this grave
tale, however, nothing seems more difficult than keeping to the
chronological order.

We have reached the point, then, in the month of August
1821, when I was living at the Hotel de Bruxelles with Lussinge,
accompanying him to dinner there every day at five o'clock
in the afternoon. M. Petit, the very nicest of Frenchmen, and
his wife, a former chambermaid who was inclined to put on
airs, although she was quite a slattern, kept a very good table.
Once I was there, Lussinge, who, as I look back on it now, was
always afraid to introduce me to his friends, could not avoid
presenting me to:

a) a most likable man, an excellent fellow, well-favored
but unenlightened, named Barot.[7] Barot was a banker from
Charleville, who was then engaged in piling up a fortune that
would bring him an annual income of 80,000 francs; and

b) an officer on half-pay named Poitevin, who had been
decorated at Waterloo, a man with absolutely no wit, and if
possible, with even less imagination, in fact a blockhead, but
a well-bred blockhead, who had had so many women that he
had become sincere at least on their account.[8]

The conversation of M. Poitevin, his unfailing good sense,
utterly free of any fanciful exaggeration, his views on women
and his advice in matters of dress were all most useful to me. I
believe the poor fellow had only 1200 francs in income and a

salary of 1500 francs from some small post, but he was never-theless one of the best dressed young men in Paris. Of course he never went out without spending two and a half hours on his toilette. Finally, as I remember, he had a passing love affair, of a couple of months duration, with the Marquise des Rosine, to whom I was later beholden for so much.[9]

On at least a dozen occasions I swore I would have her myself, but I never made the attempt, which was doubtless wrong of me. She forgave me my ugliness, and I certainly owed it to her to become her lover. When I next go to Paris I must see about paying this debt. She may be more responsive to my attentions since we are neither of us very young any more. But perhaps I am boasting a bit, for she has been very well-behaved during the last ten years, though against her will, as I see it.

At any rate I owe the most heartfelt gratitude to the mar-quise for her kindness to me after I was abandoned by Mme. Dar., on whom I must have counted so much.[10]

Only by dint of careful reflection, in order to be in the proper frame of mind to write this memoir, am I able to piece together all that passed through my heart in 1821. I have always lived and still live from day to day, without concerning myself at all with what I shall do tomorrow. The passage of time is recorded for me only by the advent of Sunday, when as a rule I am bored and take everything amiss. I have never been able to understand why. In 1821 my Sundays in Paris were quite dreadful for me. As I wandered through the Tuileries gardens, under the great chestnut-trees that were so majes-tic at that season of the year, I would think of Metilda, who always made it a point to spend that day at the home of her cousin, the wealthy Mme. Traversi. Though she hated me, this sinister woman was envious of her cousin, and together with her friends persuaded Metilda that she would disgrace herself utterly if she took me for her lover.

Whenever I was not in the company of my three friends, Lussinge, Barot and Poitevin, I would sink into gloomy reverie. In reality I accepted their society only to get away from my own thoughts. The pleasure of being distracted from my sufferings for a moment, or my reluctance to be so distracted, governed all my actions at that time. Whenever one of these gentlemen suspected me of being melancholy, I would begin to prattle about the first thing that came into my head, sometimes uttering the most arrant nonsense, and saying things that above all should never be said in France, because they offend the vanity of the listener. M. Poitevin made me suffer for such quips many times over.

I have never been discreet about what I say; I talk too much at random. Since I spoke only to assuage for the moment my poignant grief, endeavoring to conceal the fact that I had parted from a beloved friend in Milan, and that this was the cause of my wretchedness—which, if they had known, would have provoked jests at the expense of my presumed mistress that I could not have borne—I must really have appeared mad to those three prosaic and wholly unimaginative men. Several years later I heard that they considered me extremely affected. As I write this now, I realize that if chance, or perhaps a particle of worldly wisdom had led me to seek out the company of women, I might have met with success, I might have found some consolation, despite my age, my ugliness, etc. I had a mistress only by accident, in 1824, three years later. By then the memory of Metilda was no longer so harrowing. She became a sort of spectral creature for me, sweet and profoundly sad, whose apparition evoked all sorts of tender, just, noble and generous notions in my mind.

I found it a painful ordeal in 1821 to return for the first time in many long years to the houses where I had been so kindly received when I was at the court of Napoleon.*

I kept putting it off again and again. At length my presence in Paris became known, as I was obliged to shake hands with friends I met in the street. People complained that I was neglecting them.

The Count d'Argout, my associate when we were both auditors at the Council of State, an excellent fellow and a tireless worker, although far from nimble-witted, was a peer of France in 1821. It was he who gave me a ticket for the Hall of Peers, where the trial of some poor wretches charged with conspiracy was being held. The case of these impulsive, irrational bunglers, as I remember, was called the conspiracy of August 19th or 20th. It was a lucky accident for them that their heads did not fall. There, for the first time, I saw M. Odilon Barot, a little man with a blue beard.[11]

Barot was defending one of the poor fools who had become involved in the conspiracy, while possessing only two-thirds or three-quarters of the courage necessary for such a wild undertaking. The logic of M. Odilon Barot impressed me. As a rule I took my place a few steps behind the chair of the Chancellor, M. d'Ambray, who seemed to me to be conducting the proceedings with great propriety, considering that he was an aristocrat.†

The Chancellor had the bearing and manners of M. Petit, the major-domo at the Hotel de Bruxelles, but with this differ-

---

* *There* give details of those circles.—*Beyle.*
† Here a description of the Hall of Peers.—*Beyle.*

ence, that M. d'Ambray's manners were less aristocratic than those of the former valet of the Damas brothers. The next day I spoke in praise of his judicial qualities at the home of the Countess Doligny.[12]

The mistress of M. d'Ambray happened to be present there. She was a plump woman of thirty-six, with a fresh complexion and the easy carriage of Mlle. Contat in her last years. (Mlle. Contat was an inimitable actress whose career I followed eagerly in 1803, I believe.)

I made a mistake not to become intimate with M. d'Ambray's mistress. My wild talk gave me some distinction in her eyes. But she thought I was the lover, or one of the lovers, of Mme. Doligny. With her I might have found the remedy for my troubles, but I was blind.

One day as I was leaving the Hall of Peers I met my cousin, Baron Martial Daru. He still clung to his title,[13] but in other respects he was the best fellow in the world, my benefactor, indeed the preceptor who taught me what little I know of how to conduct myself with women, first in Milan in 1800, and then in Brunswick in 1807.

In his time he had twenty-two mistresses, and always the prettiest, always the best to be found wherever he happened to be. It was I who burned all their portraits, locks of hair, etc.[14]

"I say! How long have you been in Paris?"

"Three days."

"Come to our house tomorrow. My brother will be very glad to see you."

And how did I respond to this warm and friendly welcome? I let six or seven years go by before I went to pay my respects to these worthy relatives of mine. Indeed I was so ashamed of my negligence in this regard that up to the date of their premature death I called on them no more than ten times in all. My kind friend Martial Daru died around 1829, after having grown heavy and insipid as a result of taking aphrodisiac potions, on the subject of which I had two or three scenes with him. A few months later, while sitting in the Café du Rouen, then at the corner of the rue du Rempart, I was prostrated when I read in my newspaper of the death of Count Daru. With tears in my eyes I jumped into a cab and drove to 81 rue de Grenelle. The lackey who came to the door was weeping, and I too shed scalding tears. I knew I had been an ungrateful wretch, and I capped my ingratitude by leaving that very evening for Italy, as I recall, hastening my departure, in fact, for I should have died of grief if I had entered his house at the time. In this action too there was a trace of the folly that made me seem so baroque in 1821.

The son of M. Doligny also defended one of the conspirators on trial. From the place he occupied at the counselors' table he caught sight of me, and I could not get out of calling on his mother. She was a woman, and a woman of strong character as well; I do not know why I did not take advantage of the warmth with which she received me to tell her my troubles and ask her advice. There again happiness was within my reach, for the voice of reason from the mouth of a woman would have had far more influence over me than my own efforts at logic.

I often took dinner with Mme. Doligny. The second or third time I dined with her she invited me to lunch with the mistress of M. d'Ambray, then chancellor. Although I was well-received, I was too stupid to become an intimate of that friendly circle. Whether as an accepted or as a cast-off lover I might have found a little *forgetfulness* there, which is what I was searching for everywhere, for example, in my long solitary walks in Montmartre or the Bois de Boulogne. I was so unhappy at the time that since then I have developed a perfect horror for those pleasant regions. But I was blind. It was not until 1824, when by chance I acquired a mistress, that I found the cure for my troubles.

What I am writing seems very dull to me; if this continues it will not be a book but an examination of conscience. I remember few details of that period of storm and passion.

Seeing my wretched conspirators daily at the Hall of Peers inspired me with one striking thought: To fight a duel with someone you have never spoken to must be a dull business. How could any of these boobies have got the idea of imitating L . . . ?[15]

My recollection of that period is so vague that I really am uncertain whether it was in 1814 or in 1821 that I met the mistress of M. d'Ambray at the home of Mme. Doligny.

It seems to me now that in 1821 I only saw the Dolignys at their chateau in Corbeil, and at that I could not bring myself to go there except after several pressing invitations.

Chapter III

Through being in love in 1821 I acquired a very comic virtue: that of chastity.

Against my will, my friends Lussinge, Barot and Poitevin, finding me low in spirits, arranged a delightful evening at a bordello for my benefit in August 1821. From what I have learned since, Barot is one of the best qualified men in Paris to organize an entertainment of this kind, a somewhat delicate business. A woman is a woman for him only once: the first time. He lives on 30,000 of his 80,000 francs a year, and of this 30,000 he spends at least 20,000 on wenches.

Barot therefore made all the arrangements for an evening at the establishment of Mme. Petit, one of his former mistresses, to whom, I believe, he had recently lent some money to set up a house of pleasure *(to raise a brothel)*[1] in the Rue du Cadran, at the corner of the rue Montmartre, on the fourth floor.

We were to have Alexandrine—who six months later was being kept by the wealthiest Englishmen in town—then only a novice of two months' experience. We arrived at eight o'clock in the evening, and toiling up four flights of stairs found a charming reception room, champagne in ice buckets, hot punch . . . At length Alexandrine was led in under the surveillance of a lady's maid. I have forgotten now who had engaged this lady's maid, but she must have had considerable authority, for I saw on the bill for the evening's entertainment that she was put down for twenty francs. When Alexandrine appeared she surpassed everyone's expectations. She was a tall lass of sixteen or seventeen, already well-formed, with the same black eyes that I found later in the portrait of the Duchess of Urbino by Titian in the museum at Florence. But for the color of her hair, she was the image of Titian's portrait. She was a gentle, healthy creature, a bit shy but cheerful, and decorous withal. The eyes of my colleagues started from their heads at the mere sight of her. Lussinge offered her a glass of champagne, which she refused; he then retired with her. Mme. Petit brought in two other girls. They were not bad, but we told her that she herself was a prettier woman. She had indeed a very trim foot. Poitevin carried her off. After a frightful interval Lussinge returned, his face quite pale.

"Your turn, Beyle. Good luck!" they cried.

I found Alexandrine stretched out in bed, a little wan, in almost the same costume and in precisely the same position as the Duchess of Urbino in Titian's portrait.

"Let's chat for a few minutes," she said sensibly. "I'm a bit tired. Let's talk. In a little while I'll regain my former ardor."

She was adorable. I doubt that I have ever seen anyone so lovely. She was not too wanton, except that gradually her eyes began to light up with excitement, one might even say with passion.

I failed her completely; it was a perfect *fiasco*. I then tried to make amends in another way, and she seemed to countenance it. Not knowing exactly what to do next, I tried to go on with my sleight of hand, but she put a stop to it. She seemed astonished at my behavior. I then said a few words to cover my confusion and left the room.

Barot had scarcely succeeded me when we heard shouts of laughter that reached us from the other end of the apartment. Suddenly Mme. Petit dismissed the other girls and Barot led Alexandrine into the room, dressed

> *. . . dans le simple appareil*
> *D'une beauté qu'on vient d'arracher au sommeil.*[2]

"My great admiration for Beyle," said Barot, roaring with laughter, "makes me want to imitate him. I come to fortify myself with champagne." They could not stop laughing for ten minutes. Poitevin rolled on the floor. Alexandrine's wide-eyed astonishment was priceless to behold. It was the first time anyone had failed the poor girl.

My friends expected me to feel mortally ashamed, and tried to persuade me that this was the unhappiest moment of my life. But as a matter of fact, I was merely surprised, nothing more. Somehow the thought of Metilda had come to me as I was entering the room so charmingly adorned by Alexandrine.

At any rate, I doubt if I resorted to harlots more than three times in the ten years that followed. The first time after my encounter with the delightful Alexandrine was in October or November of 1826, in a moment of great despair.

Thereafter I frequently ran into Alexandrine driving about in the sumptuous equipage she acquired only a month later, and she always had a glance of recognition for me. But after five or six years of that kind of life her face grew coarse, like all women of her class.

From that moment on I passed for a *Babillan* in the minds of my three boon companions. My fine reputation became a subject of gossip in society, and endured in one form or another until Mme. Azur was able to give a different account of my powers.[3]

My relations with Barot, meanwhile, were improved by the events of that evening. I still like him and he likes me. He is probably the only Frenchman with whom I can enjoy passing two weeks in his country place. He has the most loyal heart, the frankest disposition, and at the same time the least discernment and education of any man I know. But in two fields he is supreme: that of making money without playing the stock market, and that of striking up an acquaintance with strange women on the street or at the theatre, above all in the second department.

This is an absolute necessity for him, because any woman who once gives him her favors thereafter means no more to him than a man.

One evening in Milan Metilda was speaking to me of her friend Mme. Bignami. Of her own accord she began to tell me of one of Mme. Bignami's love affairs, adding: "Imagine her hard lot; every evening after her lover bade her goodnight he went off to a harlot."

Only after I left Milan did I realize that this moral observation had nothing to do with the story of Mme. Bignami, but was intended as a rebuke to me.

In truth, every evening after I had accompanied Metilda to the house of her cousin, Mme. Traversi, to whom I had boorishly refused to be presented, I used to go to pass the rest of the evening with the charming, the divine Countess Kassera. And here I made another blunder, of a piece with my conduct toward Alexandrine, for I once refused to be the lover of the Countess Kassera, who was one of the most delectable women I have ever known, only in order to merit the love of Metilda in the eyes of God! In the same spirit and for the same reason

I refused the advances of the celebrated Mme. Vigano, who, as she was descending the stairs[4] with all her retinue—and among her courtiers was that witty and reasonable fellow, Count Saurau[5]—dropped behind the to say to me:

"Beyle, they say that you are in love with me?"

"They are mistaken," I answered very coldly, without even kissing her hand.

Such infamous behavior to a woman who was accustomed to having her own way, earned me her implacable hatred. She would never greet me again, even when we met face to face in one of the narrow streets of Milan.

Those are my three great blunders. I shall never forgive myself for my stupidity with regard to Countess Kassera (today she is the most respectable and most respected woman in her country).

CHAPTER IV

HERE IS ANOTHER CIRCLE WITH WHICH I WAS FAMILIAR, in contrast with that described in the preceding chapter.

One day in 1817, the man whose writings I most admired, the only man in fact who ever succeeded in overturning my ideas, Count de Tracy, came to see me at the Hotel d'Italie in the Place Favart. I have never been so surprised in my life. For a dozen years I had revered his *Idéologie*, for which he will one day be famous. He called on me because someone had given him a copy of my *Histoire de la Peinture en Italie*.

He spent an hour with me. I admired him so much that I probably cut a poor figure on this occasion, a *fiasco* due to excessive love. Never did I think less of trying to appear witty or agreeable. I strove rather to approach that vast intellect; I looked on it in awe; I asked only for light. Besides, at that period, I had not yet learned how to *be witty*.

This form of improvisation, possible only to a tranquil mind, did not come to me until 1827.[1]

M. Destutt de Tracy, peer of France, member of the Academy, was a little old man with a trim and elegant figure, but of a somewhat singular appearance. He always wore a green visor, on the pretext that he was blind.[2]

In 1811, as I remember, I was present when he was installed in the Academy by M. de Ségur, whose address of welcome, in the name of the imperial despotism, was full of nonsense. Although I myself was attached to the court at the time, I was disgusted by the exhibition. We are going to sink into military barbarism, I said to myself, we are all going to become like General Grosse.[3]

This General Grosse, whom I met at the home of Countess Daru, was one of the most witless swashbucklers of the Imperial Guard—which is saying a great deal. In his Provençal accent he used to boast of his longing to run his sabre through all Frenchmen opposed to the man who gave him his provender. This sort of spirit became my pet aversion, to such a degree that in the afternoon of the battle of the Moscow River, when I came on the remains of several generals of the Imperial Guard, I could not keep from exclaiming: "Now there are a few less braggarts in the world!" A remark that almost did for me, and seemed inhuman to those who overheard me.

M. de Tracy has never consented to have his portrait painted. To my mind he resembles Pope Clement, of the Corsini family, whose bust may be seen at Santa Maria Maggiore, in the beautiful chapel to the left of the entrance.[4]

His manners are perfect, except when he falls into one of his abominable black humors. I was not able to figure out his true character until 1822. He is in reality an old Don Juan (see Mozart's opera, Molière, etc.). A trifle can put him out of sorts. For instance, in his own drawing-room, M. de Lafayette outranked him a bit as a great man. In the second place, his compatriots did not appreciate his *Idéologie* or his *Logique*. The exquisite little rhetoricians of the Academy only admitted him to their ranks as the author of a good grammar, and then he was duly reviled by the vapid M. de Ségur, father of an even more vapid son (Philippe de Ségur, who wrote of our misfortunes in Russia in such a way as to win a decoration from Louis XVIII). The infamous Philippe is an example of the kind of character I detest most in Paris: a defender of the government, a man of honor always, except in the decisive issues of our time.

Of late Philippe has been playing the same role with regard to Casimir Périer, the cabinet minister (see the *Journal des Débats* of May 1832) that formerly won him the favor of Napoleon, whom he so basely abandoned to seek the favor of Louis XVIII. The king enjoyed having degraded characters of this type around him, for he understood their baseness perfectly, and used to make sly allusions whenever he caught them making some noble gesture. Perhaps that friend of Favras, he who waited to hear the news of Favras' hanging before declaring to one of his gentlemen-in-waiting: "Let us be served!" was conscious of possessing such a character himself. He was just the man to admit that he was a knave and to laugh at his own infamy.[5]

I am aware that the term "infamy" is not quite apt in the case of Philippe de Ségur, but I have a deep-rooted antipathy for his peculiar type of perfidy. I respect a gallows-bird infinitely more, a simple murderer who gives way to a moment's weakness, and who, besides, has never eaten a square meal in his life. In 1828 or thereabouts, our fine Philippe seduced and got with child a very rich widow, who was obliged to marry him (Mme. Gréfulhe, widow of a peer of France). I used to dine with him occasionally when he was a general in the service of the emperor. At that time he talked of nothing but his thirteen war wounds, for the beast has courage.

I suppose he would be considered a hero in Russia, or in any one of those half-civilized countries, but in France people are beginning to understand his low character. My friends Mme.

Garnett and her daughter-in-law (Rue Duphot, No. 12) offered to bring me to the house of his brother, who lived next door at No. 14, I believe, but I always refused the invitation because of my hatred for the historian of the Russian campaign.

His father, Count Ségur, who was Grand Master of Ceremonies at Saint-Cloud when I was stationed there, never got over his disappointment at not having been made a duke. In his view it was worse than a misfortune; it was unseemly. All his ideas were *stunted,* and he had a great quantity of them, of all kinds. He saw traces of vulgarity in everyone and everything, and with what refinement did he not express his own sentiments!

The one thing I liked in the poor creature was that his wife loved him passionately. For the rest, whenever I had occasion to speak to him I felt as if I were dealing with a Lilliputian.

I used to run into M. de Ségur, who was Grand Master of Ceremonies from 1810 to 1814, at the homes of several of Napoleon's ministers. Since the fall of the great man, of whom he was one of the weaknesses and one of the misfortunes, I have not met him once.

Even the Dangeaus[6] at the Emperor's court, and there were many of them, as for instance my friend Baron Martial Daru, even men of that kind were unable to restrain their laughter at the elaborate ceremonial devised by the Count de Ségur for Napoleon's marriage to Marie-Louise of Austria, and especially for their first meeting.

However infatuated he may have been with his new royal vestments, Napoleon found Ségur's ritual absurd, and laughed over it with Duroc, who told me the story. I believe that none of those labyrinthine details were ever carried out. If I had with me here all the papers I left in Paris, I should insert Ségur's programme for the marriage festivities in these nonsensical reminiscences. It makes admirable reading; in fact it sounds like a hoax.

But now in 1832 I sigh and say to myself: "See how low Napoleon, an Italian, was brought by the petty vanity of Paris!"

Where was I? . . . Heavens, how badly written this is!

M. de Ségur used to be particularly sublime at the meetings of the Council of State. This Council was a respectable body. In 1810 it was not, as its counterpart is today (1832) an assemblage of vulgar pedants such as Cousin, Jacqueminot, and others even more obscure.

Except for the bigwigs who were his fierce enemies, Napoleon had brought together the fifty least stupid men of France in his Council of State. It was divided into sections. Sometimes the war section (in which I served my apprenticeship under the admirable Gouvion de Saint-Cyr), met with the section of the Interior, over which M. de Ségur occasionally presided. How he happened to be there I do not recall, but it might have been during the absence or illness of Regnault (of Saint-Jean d'Angely), an energetic man.

JUNE 23.

When faced with a difficult problem, such as the levying of troops for the guard of honor in Piedmont, on which occasion I happened to be one of the humble recording secretaries, the elegant and polished M. de Ségur, for lack of a better idea, would hitch his chair forward with an incredibly comical movement, by gripping it between his outspread thighs.

But after laughing at his ineptitude, I would ask myself: "Can it be that I am at fault, and not he? After all, this man won some fame as ambassador to the court of Catherine the Great, and once stole the pen of the British Ambassador.[7] He is also the author of a history of the reign of William II or III (I don't remember which at this moment, but at any rate the lover of Mme. Lichtenau, for whom Benjamin Constant fought a duel)."

In my youth I was inclined to *feel too much respect* for certain figures. When my imagination seized on a man, I would be struck dumb before him; *I adored his faults.* But the absurdity of M. de Ségur acting as social mentor to Napoleon proved, it would seem, too much even for my gallibility.[8]

Aside from such matters, the Count de Ségur was a man from whom you might seek counsel on the most delicate matters of personal conduct, even regarding women, when he could perform like a hero. He was likewise capable of saying delicate and charming things, but only at the Lilliputian level of his own mentality.

I made a great mistake not to cultivate that amiable old man between 1821 and 1830. He died, I believe, at the same time as his good wife. But I was mad; my loathing for all that seemed *vile* used to cause me veritable agony, instead of furnishing me with a source of amusement, as it does today, when I behold the conduct of those at the court of . . .[9]

On my return from England in 1817, Count de Ségur sent me his compliments on my little book *Rome, Naples et Florence,* which I had presented to him.

At heart I have always scorned Paris on moral grounds. To succeed in Paris one ought to be a grand master of ceremonies, like M. de Ségur.

On physical grounds as well Paris was never attractive to me. Even on my first visit, around 1803, I was frightfully disappointed because it was not surrounded by mountains. The mountains of my native region (Dauphiné) which for the first sixteen years of my life were the silent witnesses of my deepest emotions, gave me a *bias* (an English term meaning "bent") that I have never lost.

It was only on July 28, 1830 that I began to have any respect for Paris.[10]

Even when the shooting began, the day of the Ordinances,[11] as late as eleven o'clock in the evening, I made fun of the courage of the Parisians and of the resistance that might be expected of them.

I was at Count Réal's house at the time, and I suspect that that jovial fellow and his heroic daughter, Baroness Lacuée, have not yet forgiven me for what I said then.[12]

Today I have a high regard for Paris. I admit that in the matter of courage its people are in the first rank, as also for their cooking and their *wit*. But for all that it does not attract me. It seems to me that there is always a trace of *sham* even in its finer attributes. The young Parisians I know, like M. Féburier, or Viollet-le-Duc, whose fathers possessed enough manly energy to come up from the provinces and make their fortunes, appear rather *effeminate* to me, concerned only with the cut of their clothes, the elegance of their hats, or the question of how to tie their cravats. It is hard for me to conceive of a man without a little *manly energy,* without some depth and constancy in his ideas, all of which are as rare in Paris society as a vulgar turn of speech, or, for that matter, a *harsh* statement.

But I must close this chapter here. In order not to lie or conceal my faults, I have given myself the stint of writing these recollections twenty pages at a time, like a letter. After I die, they are to be printed after the original manuscript. Perhaps in this way I shall arrive at the *absolute truth,* but I must also entreat the reader (perhaps someone born this morning in the house next door) to forgive me for these frightful digressions.

Chapter V

ROME, JUNE 23, 1832.

AS FAR AS I CAN SEE IN 1832—AS A RULE MY PHILOSOPHY IS of the day of writing, and I was far from understanding this in 1821—I seem to have stood at a half-way point between the energetic vulgarity of men like General Grosse or Count Regnault de Saint-Jean d'Angely, and the rather narrow and Lilliputian graces of Count de Ségur or M. Petit, the major-domo at the Hotel de Bruxelles.

Only by the fact that I despised base actions did I diverge from the extremes here mentioned. Through want of cunning, through want of application, as M. Delécluze of the *Journal des Débats* used to say to me when speaking of my books and of my being admitted to the Institute, I missed five or six chances for a great success in politics, finance, and literature. As it happened, opportunity in each of these fields came knocking at my door in turn. But my own reveries, which in 1821 were all of love, although they later acquired a philosophical and melancholy cast (all vanity aside, exactly like that of Jacques in *As You Like It*), have come to mean so much to me that when a friend accosts me in the street, I'd gladly give him a ducat not to address a word to me. The merest glimpse of someone I know at such moments is provoking. When I see an acquaintance approaching me in the distance, and realize that I must greet him, I begin to be vexed while he is still fifty feet away. On the other hand I enjoy going out into society and meeting friends in the evening: Saturdays at M. Cuvier's, Sundays at M. de Tracy's, Tuesdays at Mme. Ancelot's, Wednesdays at Baron Gérard's, etc.

Any man with a little tact soon notices that he irritates me by hailing me in the street. His vanity tells him: there's a man who does not appreciate my worth. But that is not true.

For this reason it gives me great pleasure to step out in some foreign town (such as Lancaster or Torre del Greco) one hour after my arrival, before I am known to anyone there. For several years now I have missed this sort of thing. If I were not afraid to be seasick I would gladly go to America. Will anyone believe me? I would enjoy wearing a mask; I would be delighted to change my name. My mind is crammed with tales from the "Thousand and One Nights," and I often dream of Angelica's magic ring. It would give me the greatest satisfaction to be transformed into a tall blond German and to walk through the streets of Paris in that guise.

By turning back a few pages I see that I was on the subject of M. de Tracy. This trim little old man with the huge green eye-shade, always dressed in black, rocking from one foot to the other in front of the hearth, as I remember him, had a way of speaking that was quite the opposite of his style of writing. His conversation was made up of very subtle observations, elegantly phrased; he shrank from the use of a forceful word as from an oath. And yet he wrote like a village mayor. The energetic simplicity with which I expressed myself at that time must have been highly unpalatable to him. Besides I wore enormous black whiskers then, in fact until Mme. Doligny's raillery made me shave them off a year later. My resemblance to an Italian butcher did not seem to make a favorable impression on a man who had held the rank of colonel in the reign of Louis XVI.

M. de Tracy was born around 1765, blessed with an income of 300,000 francs a year, and was brought up by his widowed mother. His residence was on the rue de Tracy, near the rue Saint-Martin.

Like ever so many rich people in 1780, he tried to carry off some business deals without knowing the first thing about it. M. de Tracy made his street, and thereby lost some two or three hundred thousand francs, and so forth.[1]

With the result that today this man (who was such a delightful fellow when he was the lover of Mme. Praslin in 1790), this deep thinker has at most some 30,000 francs of income out of the 300,000 he began with.

His mother, a woman of rare good sense, was wrapped up in the life at court. It is not surprising therefore that at the age of twenty-two her son was commissioned colonel of a regiment. Among the captains of this regiment was another Tracy, not one whit less noble than he, his cousin, in fact, who apparently never resented for a moment the appointment of that little marionette of twenty-two to the command of the regiment in which he served.

This little marionette, so full of noble impulses, as Mme. de Tracy told me later, nevertheless had a deep core of common sense in him. His mother, a most remarkable woman, having learned that there was a certain philosopher in Strasbourg (let me point out, by the way, that this was around 1780, and that the sage in question was not as celebrated as Voltaire, Diderot or Raynal) having learned, as I was saying, that there was a philosopher in Strasbourg who analyzed men's thoughts, interpreting the metaphorical equivalents or symbols of all sensual and emotional experience, grasped at once that familiarity with such processes would enrich her son's mind.

Imagine what kind of mind a handsome young man like that must have had in 1785, a highborn youth brought up at court, with an income of 300,000 francs a year!

To achieve her ends the Marquise de Tracy had her son transferred to the artillery, in which branch of the service he was obliged to spend two years in succession at Strasbourg. If I ever happen to pass through that city, I shall try to find out the name of the German philosopher who had some renown there in the 1780's.

Two years later, I believe, M. de Tracy was at Rethel with his regiment, which, I recall, was then the Royal Dragoons, a fact I must verify in the Court Calendar of the time.

Lemons . . .

It was not M. de Tracy who spoke to me about those lemons; I heard the story from another misanthrope, a M. Jacquemont, a former monk, and furthermore a man of the highest merit. But M. de Tracy told me many other anecdotes about the reorganized French Army, of which M. de Lafayette was commander-in-chief.

His lieutenant-colonel wanted to take over the regiment and have the men emigrate in a body . . .

Leave of absence and duel . . .[2]

A tall figure, surmounted by a cold, imperturbable face, as meaningless as an old family portrait, the bumpy head covered by a short, ill-fitting periwig, the huge body clad in a nondescript, shapeless gray coat, such was General de Lafayette as he came limping into Mme. de Tracy's drawing-room, leaning on his cane, just as the Gascon artist Scheffer caught him in his strikingly accurate portrait. Mme. de Tracy always addressed him as *my dear Sir,* in her flutiest tone.

This *dear Sir* of Mme. de Tracy, spoken in that reverent tone, made M. de Tracy a bit uncomfortable, I suspect, not because M. de Lafayette might have been on too intimate terms with his wife—at his age he was probably indifferent to troubles of that kind—but simply because Mme. de Tracy's sincere admiration for M. de Lafayette, an admiration that was never feigned or exaggerated, made it only too evident that the general was the leading figure of her salon.

However immature I may have been in 1821 (I have always lived in my illusions of enthusiasm and passion) I was able to distinguish this nuance *all by myself.*

I also felt, without needing to be told, that M. de Lafayette was quite simply a hero out of Plutarch. He lived from day to day, without much understanding, performing the great deed required of him at the moment, like Epaminondas.

Meanwhile, despite his great age (he was born in 1757, the same year as Charles X, with whom he used to play court tennis as a youth) he was mainly concerned with plucking at the skirt of some pretty girl from behind (*vulgo:* to goose). This he did as often as possible and without standing on much ceremony.

While awaiting an opportunity to perform great deeds, which of course do not present themselves every day, and also watching out for a chance to pinch the young women, which was possible only at half-past twelve when they took their leave, M. de Lafayette used to expound all the common-place ideas of the National Guard in a rather crude way. He would say: Only that government is good which guarantees the safety of its citizens on the highway, equality before the law, an enlightened judiciary, sound money, good roads, and the protection of foreigners. Stated this way, the whole matter is not very complicated.

It must be admitted, however, that there is a vast difference between a man like Lafayette and M. de Ségur, the Grand Master of Ceremonies. In the years to come, France, and Paris in particular, will be execrated by posterity for not having recognized this man's true greatness.

As for me, accustomed as I was to Napoleon and Lord Byron, to whom I might add the names of Lord Brougham, Monti, Canova and Rossini, I recognized the veritable greatness of M. de Lafayette at once, and I stand by that judgment.

During the July days I saw him in action, with his shirt all torn. True, he encouraged all the schemers, all the blockheads, all those who tended to be bombastic. To me he was less cordial; at one time he demanded that I be sacked (in favor of his boorish secretary, M. Levasseur). Yet it never entered my head to be angry at him or to venerate him any the less, any more than it would occur to me to curse the sun because it was hidden by a cloud.[3]

At the tender age of seventy-five, M. de Lafayette had the same frailties that I had. He was mad about a young Portuguese girl of eighteen who turned up in Mme. de Tracy's salon, a friend of his granddaughters, in fact, of Mlle. Georges Lafayette, Mlle. de Lasteyrie, and Mlle. de Maubourg. He fancied that the young Portuguese, although it might have been any other young woman there, had singled him out for her favors. He could think of nothing else. And the amusing thing is that he was often right about this. His international fame, the natural elegance of his speech, despite its apparent simplicity, the sparkle in his eyes as soon as they discerned a pretty bosom, everything contributed to making his last years pass merrily enough, to the great disapproval of certain women of thirty-five, such as the Marquise de Marmier (Choiseul), Mme. de Perret, and others who frequented the Tracy salon. Women of that type cannot conceive of any other way of being charming than by mouthing the precious little phrases of a M. de Ségur or the glittering aphorisms of a Benjamin Constant.

M. de Lafayette is extremely courteous and even affectionate towards everyone, but *courteous in the manner of a king.* When I said this to Mme. de Tracy one day, she grew as angry as a woman could who was sweetness itself; but perhaps thereafter she was able to distinguish between the vigorous simplicity of my discourse and the stupidity of someone like Dunoyer. Dunoyer, who is today the upright prefect of Moulins, was a good liberal, one of the best intentioned, perhaps the most heroic, as well as the dullest of the liberal writers. Let no one doubt me, since I belong to that party, but this is saying a good deal. Dunoyer, the editor of the *Censeur,*[4] and two or three other men of the same stripe, used to hang over the general's armchair in open-mouthed hero-worship.

They were rudely shocked however when he gave them the slip at the first opportunity, and went off to admire at close quarters the lovely shoulders of some young woman who had just walked in, his eyes glowing. These poor men of *virtue* (all of whom, by the way, sold out to Périer, the prime minister, in 1832) looked so doleful when they were thus abandoned that I used to poke fun at them, to the great scandal of my new lady-love. But it was understood that she had a weakness for me. "There is a certain *spark in him,*" she said one day to another woman, one of those who admired the trivial Lilliputian sayings of men like Ségur. This other woman had complained of the frankness and severity with which I had said that although the ultra-liberals there were doubtless to be respected for their great virtue, they were utterly incapable of comprehending that two and two make four. Dunoyer and his friends were so slow and heavy, for all their virtue, they were so quick to take fright at the merest hint of plain talk to the "American party," that it was really incredible. Neither were there any ideas above the level of the commonplace in men like Ludovic Vietet and Mortimer Ternaux, members of the younger generation who brought new blood into the Tracy salon around 1826. Of all these M. de Lafayette was and probably still is the *party leader.*

He must have learned all the tricks of the trade in 1789. To be a party leader, you must not alienate anyone, and you must remember everyone's name. In these respects M. de Lafayette excels. The artificial and pressing interests of a party leader make him fight shy of any *literary ideas,* of which, in any case, I suspect he is incapable. It is probably for this reason that he is not aware of the heaviness and dullness of M. Dunoyer and his associates.*

JUNE 24, 1832

I have forgotten to describe the Tracy drawing-room. Sir Walter Scott and his imitators would have used that as a point of departure, but I detest physical descriptions. It is because I find it such a bore that I am reluctant to write novels.

---

* June 23, 1832, third day of work, from [pages] 60 to 90.—*Beyle.*

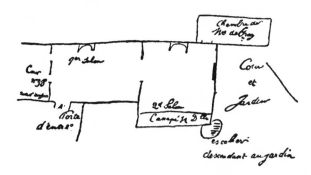

Through the doorway A you enter a long drawing room, at the farther end of which is a large double door, always ajar. Beyond this is a big square salon with a handsome chandelier and a wretched little clock on the mantelpiece. On the right as you enter this room there is a broad blue divan where a bevy of girls from twelve to eighteen years old are seated beside their suitors. Among these is M. Charles de Remusat, who is quite witty and even more affected—a counterpart of the famous actor, Fleury. Another is M. François de Corcelles, who has all the candor and ruggedness of a republican. It is quite likely that he sold out in 1831, for in 1820 he had already published a little book that had the ill-luck to win the praise of M. Dupin, the lawyer (a confirmed rascal and known by me to be such since 1827). But in 1821 Remusat and Corcelles were considered quite remarkable, and since that time they have each married one of M. de Lafayette's granddaughters. Hovering nearby M. Scheffer, the painter, was generally to be found, a cold Gascon, who in my opinion is the most brazen liar and has the meanest face of any man I know.

I was once told that he had paid court to the divine [Virginie], the oldest of M. de Lafayette's granddaughters, who has since married the eldest son of M. Augustin Périer, the most important and the most ponderous of my fellow townsmen in Grenoble. Mlle. Virginie was the favorite of Mme. de Tracy, I suspect.

Near the elegant M. de Remusat there were usually two Jesuitical gentlemen with a false and shifty look. These men, who were brothers, enjoyed the privilege of talking to Count de Tracy for hours at a stretch. I admired them greatly, with all the ardor of my youth (in the matter of concealing my affection I had barely reached the age of twenty-one in 1821). Having appraised them quickly, I felt my respect for M. de Tracy diminishing considerably.

Of these two brothers the elder, M. Thierry of the Academy of Inscriptions, has published a rather sentimental life of William the Conqueror. His great achievement was to restore the correct spelling of names like Clovis, Chilpéric, Thierry and other shadowy figures of our early history. He has also published a less sentimental volume on the organization of the French communes in 1200 A.D. A vice he contracted as a schoolboy has made him blind. His brother, who is much more of a Jesuit (at heart and in his behavior too) although an ultra-liberal like the other one, became prefect of Vésoul in 1830, and probably sold out in order to hold on to his salary, like his patron, M. Guizot.

In perfect contrast with these two Jesuitical brothers, with the tedious Dunoyer and the exquisite Remusat, was young Victor Jacquemont, who has since traveled widely in India. Almost six feet tall, Victor was very thin in those days. He was a misanthropic fellow, as a result of being always quite illogical; in fact, under the illusion that he was very clever, he never took the trouble to reason anything out. Typically French, he looked on any suggestion that he use his reason as an insult. Travel was therefore the only door that his vanity left open for the discovery of the truth. Nevertheless, I may be mistaken about him. I consider Victor a man of the greatest distinction, just as a connoisseur (please forgive me for using that word) sees the promise of a fine horse in a four-month-old colt that is still all legs. He became my good friend, and this very morning (1832) I have received a letter he wrote me from Kashmir, in India.[5]

There was but one defect in his nature, his envy of Napoleon, the contemptible jealousy of a subaltern for his superior. A similar envy, by the way, was the only strong feeling I ever observed in Count de Tracy. With ineffable delight the old metaphysician and Victor used to tell the anecdote of the rabbit hunt to which M. de Talleyrand once invited Napoleon, who at that time had been First Consul for only six weeks, but who was already dreaming of modeling himself after Louis XIV.

Domesticated rabbits and pigs in the Bois de Boulogne.[6]

Victor had another failing also; he was head over heels in love with Mme. Lavenelle, the wife of a police spy with an income of 40,000 francs a year, who was charged with reporting to the Tuileries everything that General Lafayette said and did. The joke was that the General, as well as Benjamin Constant and M. Brignon, used to confide all their liberal ideas to this M. Lavenelle. What made him so transparent was that he had been a terrorist in '93, and was forever talking about marching on the palace to massacre all the Bourbons. His wife was so very free-spoken and erotic in disposition that she gave me a revulsion for all *bawdy quips* in French. I enjoy that kind of talk in Italian, but even as a raw youth, when I was a second lieutenant in the 6th Dragoons, I used to be outraged at hearing such expressions in the mouth of Mme. Henriette, the captain's lady. Mme. Lavenelle was as dry as a stick, and besides she had no wit, and was incapable of real *passion;* the only thing that could excite her was a glimpse of the handsome thighs of a company of grenadiers in white cashmere breeches as they marched through the Tuileries Gardens.

Of quite another stamp was Mme. Baraguey d'Hilliers, whom I met shortly afterwards at Mme. Beugnot's house. Likewise Mme. Ruga and Mme. Aresi, friends of mine in Milan. In a word, I loathe bawdy remarks in the French tongue; the mixture of humor and emotion chills my soul, just as the sound of a knife cutting through cork offends my ear.

The description of the intellectual atmosphere of this salon is perhaps long-drawn out, but there are only two or three persons to be accounted for.

There was the delightful Louise Letort, the daughter of General Letort of the Dragoons, whom I knew well at Vienna in 1809. Mlle. Louise, who has grown up to be a beauty, without any affectation, a high-minded young woman in fact, was born on the eve or the day after Waterloo. Her mother was the charming Miss Sarah Newton, whose second husband was Mr. Victor de Tracy, son of the peer, then a major in the infantry.

We used to call M. Victor de Tracy "ramrod," which defines his character precisely. A brave fellow, wounded several times in Spain when fighting under Napoleon, he had the unfortunate habit of seeing only the dark side of things.

Just a week ago (June 1832) King Louis-Philippe dissolved the artillery regiment of the National Guard that was under the command of M. Victor de Tracy. As a deputy he is frequently heard on the rostrum, but he makes the mistake of being too polite in his speeches. One suspects that he is afraid to speak right out. He used to share his father's petty jealousy of Napoleon, but now that the hero is dead, he is changing his tune. But Napoleon was still living when I made my first appearance in the salon of the Rue d'Anjou. I saw them all rejoicing there at the news of his death, I caught the glances that seemed to say: "We always knew that an upstart, a bourgeois monarch would come to no good end."

For ten years I frequented that drawing-room. I was received with great courtesy, I was held in some esteem, but as time went on I grew less rather than more *intimate* with the people there, except for my close friends. This is another defect in my character, a defect that makes it impossible for me to blame others for my not rising in the world. But let it be understood that I am quite happy in an inferior position, despite what General Duroc has told me on several occasions about my military talents. Particularly happy, I might add, when there are two hundred leagues separating me from my chief, as now.

If my book is not too boring to interest the reader, it is therefore my hope that he will not find in it any rancor against mankind. To catch the favor of men in your behalf you must use a certain kind of bait. When I want to avail myself of their goodwill, I fish about for a good word or two, but my hand tires quickly of the fishing-rod. However, in 1814, when Napoleon appointed me to the 7th Division, Countess Daru, whose husband was then a minister, said to me: "If not for this cursed invasion, you would have been named prefect of a large city." I had some reason to believe that Toulouse was the city she had in mind.

I have left out one rather odd character in the Tracy circle, a woman I antagonized by neglecting to make myself agreeable to her. Mme. de Montcertin, a tall woman with a fine figure, but essentially timid and indolent, was a perfect creature of habit.[7]

She had two lovers, one for the city, the other for the country, both equally ungainly. This arrangement lasted I don't know how many years. It was Scheffer, the painter, as I recall, who was her country lover; her city lover was then Colonel, now General Carbonnel, who had taken it upon himself to act as personal bodyguard of General Lafayette.

One day the eight or ten nieces of Mme. de Montcertin asked her: "What is love?" To which she replied: "It is a low, vile thing, of which chambermaids are sometimes accused, and when they are guilty, we send them packing."

I should have paid court to Mme. Montcertin. There was no danger in it, and I should never have succeeded, for she was satisfied with her two men and lived in dread of becoming pregnant. But I looked on her as just a *thing,* not a human being. For this she paid me back by repeating some three or four times a week that I was a lightheaded fellow, just short of mad. At the Tracys she used to pour the tea, and it is quite true that on many occasions I never addressed a single word to her in the course of the entire evening except when she offered me a cup.

There were so many persons to whom I had to pay my respects on entering the drawing room that my heart used to fail me.

Besides the fifteen or twenty granddaughters of M. de Lafayette or their friends, almost all with dazzling blond hair and similar features (or so it seemed to me, who had just arrived from Italy) all of them drawn up in battle order on the blue divan, I was obliged to greet the following:

Countess de Tracy, sixty-three years old; Count Tracy, sixty years old; General Lafayette, and his son George Washington Lafayette. (This last was a real citizen of the United States of America, completely unspoiled by any patrician notions.)

My friend Mme. de Tracy had a son, as I have said, M. Victor de Tracy, who was born around 1785. There was also his wife, Mme. Sarah de Tracy, a radiant young woman, a model of delicate English beauty, though a trifle too thin. There were also the two daughter of the elder Tracys: Mme. George de Lafayette and Mme. de Laubépin. I was also obliged to salute the mighty M. de Laubépin, who had written the *Mémorial*[8] in collaboration with a monk he employed as secretary. Although he was always on hand, M. de Laubépin said scarcely eight or ten words during the entire evening.

For a long while I mistook Mme. George de Lafayette for a nun whom Mme. de Tracy had taken into her household out of charity. To match her appearance, Mme. Lafayette had bigoted ideas and the asperity of a Jansenist. As a matter of fact she had at least four or five daughters, while Mme. de Maubourg, M. de Lafayette's daughter, had five or six. It took me about ten years to distinguish one face from another in that array of fair maidens, all lisping the *proper thing,* which was unutterably tiresome to me, accustomed as I was to the speaking eyes and bold character of the belles of Milan, and before that to the delightful simplicity of German women. (I had been a quartermaster at Sagan, in Silesia, and at Brunswick.)

M. de Tracy had long been the intimate friend of the celebrated Dr. Cabanis, the father of materialism as a philosophy, whose book, *Rapport du physique et du moral,* had been my Bible when I was sixteen. Mme. Cabanis and her daughter, a young woman six feet tall, but nevertheless extremely amiable, used to call on Mme. de Tracy regularly. M. de Tracy once brought me to the Cabanis house in the rue des Vieilles-Tuileries, but I was driven away because they kept the place so infernally hot. At that time I had all the nervous susceptibility of an Italian. It made me frightfully uncomfortable and giddy to sit in a room with all the doors and windows shut, in company with ten other people. Imagine what it must have been like with a blazing fire on the hearth.

I did not stress this weakness of mine sufficiently to my friends. It was the fire that made me shun the house of Mme. Cabanis. Unaware of this, M. de Tracy never forgave me for my desertion. I could have said a word of explanation to the Countess de Tracy, but at that time I was *exceedingly shy,* a fault I have not yet overcome entirely.

Tall as she was, Mlle. Cabanis longed to be married. She ended by marrying a little popinjay with a tidy wig, a M. Dupaty, who considered himself a sculptor. It was he who designed the statue of Louis XIII in the Place Royale, showing the king astride an animal that looks like a mule.

The model of this mule was actually an Arabian horse that I saw frequently at M. Dupaty's house. The poor beast used to cool his heels in a corner of the studio, where M. Dupaty gave me a royal welcome as a writer of books about Italy and as the author of a history of painting. It would be hard to find a human being more *conventional,* more devoid of warmth, originality or drive than this worthy man. Parisians are so sleek, so conscious of propriety and *good form,* that sculpture is the worst possible craft for them to attempt.

For all his polish, M. Dupaty had earlier shown himself a man of the greatest courage. He should have remained in the army.

At Mme. Cabanis' house I met a professor of Greek named Thurot, an honest fellow, but extremely bourgeois, narrow-minded, and meticulous in advancing his own little schemes.

The overweening ambition of M. Thurot was to become a member of the Academy of Inscriptions. But by one of those extraordinary contradictions so often met with, this man, who never blew his nose without thinking of how he could curry favor with someone who might have the slightest influence on his nomination to the Academy, this man, I say, was actually an *ultra-liberal.* At first this formed a link between us, but soon his wife, to whom I never addressed a word, except under compulsion, decided that I was too indiscreet.

One day when M. de Tracy and M. Thurot asked me to outline my views on politics, I alienated them both by my reply.

"If I should come to power," I said, "I would immediately reprint the books of the emigrés, which stated that Napoleon, by eliminating them from the scene, had usurped a power that was not rightfully his. Three-quarters of the emigrés are now dead, but the rest I would exile to the departments near the Pyrenees. Then I would have these four or five departments surrounded by armed forces, which, for moral effect, would bivouac in that region six months of the year. Any emigré who tried to escape would be shot without mercy.

"The estates that Napoleon returned to them I would have broken up and sold in lots no larger than two acres. The emigrés would then receive an income of from one to three thousand francs a year. They would be allowed the choice of living in a foreign country, but if they went about plotting, I would show them no pity."

While I was setting forth this plan, I could see the faces of Thurot and Tracy growing longer and longer. To their small minds, emasculated by the conventions of polite society in Paris, I seemed barbarous. But a young woman who was present there applauded my statement, and particularly the boldness with which I expressed myself. She saw in me the *Huron* (of Voltaire's novel).

The marked kindness that young woman showed me consoled me for many disappointments. I was never quite her lover. She was a great coquette, keen on finery, always talking about handsome men, and closely allied with the most brilliant social set to be found in the boxes at the Opéra Comique. I am altering the facts here somewhat in order to prevent her from being recognized. Had I had the good sense to convince her that I loved her, she would probably have been quite pleased. But the truth is that I was not so infatuated with her as to forget that I was not a handsome man. As a matter of fact she had forgotten it. On one occasion when I was on the point of leaving Paris, she said to me, in the middle of her drawing-room: "There is something I must tell you," and leading me down a passage to an antechamber, which was empty, fortunately, she gave me a hearty kiss on the mouth that I returned with ardor. But I left the next day, and the affair ended there.

But before that point had been reached, *we spoke* to each other over long years, as they say in the province of Champagne. On my request she used to give me faithful reports of all the evil things that were being said about me.

Her tone was charming, neither approving nor disapproving. I found it most delightful to have her act as my chief of police in the midst of all the rather cold love-affairs that were being carried on in Paris.

The cruelty of the remarks I heard about in this way is inconceivable. One day she told me:

"At M. de Tracy's house the other evening, M. . . . , the spy, observed: 'Ah! M. Beyle has a new coat; evidently Mme. Pasta has just come into some money.'"

This stupid quip was greatly relished by those present. M. de Tracy never forgave me for my public (but entirely innocent) attachment for the famous singer.

The sting in that story is that "Céline," who reported the spy's remark to me, was probably a trifle jealous, herself, because of my constant attendance on Mme. Pasta.[9]

For at whatever hour my evening calls elsewhere ended, I would inevitably turn up afterwards at Mme. Pasta's (at the Hotel des Lillois, No. 63, rue Richelieu, opposite the Library). At first my lodgings were only a few steps up the street, at No. 47, but I finally grew tired of the ill-humor of my porter, who was always greatly vexed when he had to open the door for me at three o'clock in the morning, and I ended by going to live in Mme. Pasta's hotel. Two weeks later I found that I had lost about 70 percent of my social standing in Mme. de Tracy's salon. My great mistake was in not consulting my good friend Mme. de Tracy before taking such a step. But my conduct at that period was extremely capricious. If I had been a marquis or a colonel, with an income of 40,000 francs a year, I should have succeeded in ruining myself.

I was passionately fond of music, not music in general, I might explain, but particularly the music of Cimarosa and Mozart. Mme. Pasta's drawing room was, besides, the meeting place of all the Milanese who came to Paris. Through them, by chance, I sometimes heard mention of the name of Metilda.

Metilda, in Milan, heard rumors that I was spending all my time with an actress. Perhaps this cured her of me completely.

But I was quite blind to all that. All summer long I used to play faro in Mme. Pasta's rooms until daybreak, never speaking myself, but entranced to hear my Milanese friends speak in their native tongue, and taking in the idea of Metilda through all my senses. Then I would go up to my pleasant room on the third floor, and with tears in my eyes correct the proofs of my essay on *Love,* which I had written in pencil at Milan, during my few lucid intervals. It was so painful for me to work over it in Paris that I never cared to revise it.

Men of letters often say: "In foreign countries a man may have ingenious thoughts, but only in France is there the art of *writing a book.*" *True,* if the sole purpose of the book is *to clarify an idea,* but not if the author hopes at the same time to make the reader feel something, or wants to represent the various shades of emotion.

The French rule applies only to a work of history, as for example *l'Histoire de la Régence,* by M. Lemontey, whose truly academic style I admire. Indeed M. Lemontey's preface might pass for a model of what I call the academic style. (He is a miserly fellow; I met him frequently at Count Beugnot's house.)

In all likelihood I should win the approval of all the blockheads if I took the trouble to set down these fragmentary memoirs in a similar style. But by writing this like a letter, thirty pages at a sitting, more or less *unconsciously,* I am doing something that is *true to life.*

Now above all I wish to be truthful. If I succeed, what a miracle that will be in this era of pretense, in a society of which three-quarters of the actors are brazen charlatans like M. Magendie, or Count Regnault de Saint-Jean d'Angely, or Baron Gérard![10]

One of the peculiarities of the Revolutionary period (1789–1832) is that a man cannot be a great success without having a certain amount of brass and even some downright charlatanism in his character. M. de Lafayette alone is above all that, for you must not confuse charlatanism with his genial manner toward everyone, which is a *weapon of the greatest importance* for a party leader.

At Mme. Cabanis' house I met another man who is most assuredly no charlatan: M. Fauriel (the former lover of Mme. Condorcet). Aside from Mérimée and myself, he is the only example known to me of "non-charlatanism," that is to say, among people who have anything to do with writing.

But M. Fauriel has no reputation. One day the bookseller Bossanges offered me fifty copies of one of his works on condition that I not only write a glowing notice of it, but also see to it that my review appeared in some newspaper or other where at the moment (though only for a fortnight) I happened to be held in good favor. I was shocked by this, and declared that I would write the article for one copy only. But shortly afterward I grew so disgusted with the idea of paying court to the group of filthy scoundrels connected with that newspaper that I stopped seeing them, and, to my regret, never wrote the article.

But this incident took place in 1826 or 1827. Let us return to 1821. M. Fauriel had been shamefully treated by Mme. Condorcet (whose charm was purely physical) and after her death he took up with a shrewish little Englishwoman, almost a hunchback, Mlle. Clarke.

That Mlle. Clarke was clever cannot be denied, but her cleverness was like the horns of the chamois, dry, hard, and twisted. M. Fauriel, who at that time had a high opinion of me, lost no time in bringing me to her house, where I discovered my friend Augustin Thierry, author of the life of William the Conqueror, enthroned as the lion of the establishment. Among the other guests I was struck by the superb head of Mme. Belloc (wife of the painter) because of her astonishing resemblance to Lord Byron, whom I then admired so much. But a sharp fellow there, who took me for a Machiavelli because I had just come from Italy, said to me: "Can't you see that you're wasting your time with Mme. Belloc? She is in love with Mlle. Montgolfier (a horrible little monster with beautiful eyes)."

I was dumbfounded, no less by the charge of Machiavellianism than by the innuendo that I was in love with Mme. Belloc, but even more by the suggestion that she made love to Mme. Montgolfier. Who knows? There may be something in it.

At the end of a year or so, Mlle. Clarke picked a quarrel with me for some absurd reason, in consequence of which I saw her no more.[11]

To my great annoyance, M. Fauriel took her part. Fauriel and Victor Jacquemont were immensely superior to all my other acquaintances during those first months in Paris after my return from Italy. The Countess de Tracy was likewise at their level, if not higher. But at bottom I always shocked or scandalized the people who knew me.

To most of my acquaintances I was either a monster or a god. Even today Mlle. Clarke and her whole circle are convinced that I am a monster, a monster of immorality above all. The reader knows how things stood with me—only once did I go to a brothel—and he may remember what success I had with Alexandrine, the harlot of beauty sublime.

JUNE 24, ST. JOHN'S DAY.

This was my routine at that period:

I rose at ten o'clock; by ten-thirty I was at the Café de Rouen, where I would meet Baron Lussinge and my cousin Colomb (a man of integrity, justice and reason, who had been the friend of my childhood).[12]

It was a pity that neither of these men understood anything of my theory of the human heart, or of how the emotions are represented in literature and music. I can discuss this subject endlessly, examining the conclusions to be drawn from every new authentic anecdote; for me it is by far the most fascinating topic of conversation in the world. Later on I discovered that Mérimée, whom I otherwise esteem so highly, also lacked interest in this kind of discourse.

On the other hand, my old friend Crozet (chief engineer of the department of Isère) excels in this sort of thing, but his wife, jealous of our friendship, succeeded in separating us a number of years ago.[13]

What a pity! If he had lived in Paris M. Crozet would have been a superior person. Marriage, and above all life in the provinces, cause a man to age surprisingly early; the mind grows slack, and any activity of the brain, which is so rarely exercised, becomes painful and at length impossible.

After partaking of an excellent cup of coffee and two buns at the Café de Rouen, I would accompany Lussinge to his office. We used to go by way of the Tuileries and the quays, stopping at every stall where prints were displayed. But once I left Lussinge, the terrible hours of the day began for me. Because of the great heat that year I would go to the Tuileries Gardens to find a cool spot under the shade of the great chestnut trees. Since I cannot forget her, would it not be best to kill myself, I wondered. My life was a burden to me.

In 1821 I still had something of a passion for Italian painting that had led me to write on the subject, in 1816 and 1817. Sometimes I would go to the Museum, for which Lussinge had procured me a ticket. But the sight of these masterpieces only made me recall the Brera Museum and Metilda more vividly.

Whenever I saw the French name corresponding to hers in a book I turned pale.

I have in fact few memories of those days, all of which seemed the same. Everything that is supposed to make Paris delightful repelled me. Although I was a liberal myself, I found the liberals there outrageously silly. In short I see that I have retained a most unpleasant impression of all that went on. Everything offended me.

I used to run into Louis XVIII all the time. Fat, ox-eyed, he was a particularly revolting sight as he drove slowly through the streets behind his six well-fed horses.

I bought several plays of Shakespeare, in the English edition, at 30 sous apiece, and took them along to read in the Tuileries Gardens, dropping my book from time to time to dream about Metilda. The thought of returning to my lonely room was harrowing.

When at last five o'clock came, I flew off to have dinner at the Hotel de Bruxelles. There I would find Lussinge, gloomy, tired, bored, the worthy Barot, the elegant Poitevin, and five or six odd fellows of a type midway between a commercial swindler and a petty intriguer. Among the other patrons I recognized M. Alpy, General Michaud's former aide-de-camp. I was amazed to discover that this Alpy, who used to fetch the general's boots, now had the rank of colonel, and was also the son-in-law of M. Kensinger, the mayor of Strasbourg, a man of great wealth, but stupid, and a supporter of the government. I never spoke either to the colonel or to his father-in-law. I was more impressed by a tall, thin, yellow-faced man who talked all the time. There was a trace of the sacred fire of Jean-Jacques Rousseau in his praise of the Bourbons, which everyone else found flat and ridiculous. This M. Courvoisier had the carnage of an Austrian army officer, the very opposite of grace. Later he became famous as the Guardian of the Seals. Lussinge had known him at Besançon.

After dinner I could still enjoy the café hour, but I can scarcely say the same for the evening promenade that ensued along the Boulevard de Gand, a crowded and dusty thorough-fare, then quite fashionable.[14]

It went against the grain for me to be in such a place, rubbing shoulders with dapper subalterns, officers of the guard, high-class harlots and ladies of the middle-class who tried to emulate them.

There I used to run into one of my boyhood friends, Count de Barral, an upstanding fellow whose grandfather had the reputation of a miser, and who at the age of thirty was beginning to show signs of the same dismal malady.[15]

In 1810, as I remember, when M. de Barral had lost everything he had at gambling, I lent him some money and induced him to go to Naples. His father, a true gentleman, then gave him an allowance of 6,000 francs a year.

When Barral returned from Naples several years later he found me living with a charming actress, who used to come to my rooms every night at half past eleven and climb into my bed. I would return at one o'clock, when we would sup on cold partridge and champagne. This liaison lasted some two or three years. Mlle. Bayreter[16] had a friend named Annette Rose, whose father was well-known as a dealer in leather breeches. Annette and her two sisters, all charming girls, had been seduced in turn by the famous actor Mole.

One of them is now the Marquise de D . . . , but Annette had sunk lower and lower, and was then living with a stockbroker. I extolled her so much to Barral that he fell in love with her. Then I persuaded Annette to leave her wretched stockjobber.

By the second day of every month Barral was always penniless, for on the first, after he had received his monthly allowance of five hundred francs at his banker's, he would lay out a hundred to take his watch out of pawn, and then proceed to lose the remaining four hundred at the gaming table. I went to the trouble of giving two dinners to the opposing parties at Very's, in the Tuileries Gardens, and at length induced Annette to become Count Barral's steward, to live with him economically on the five hundred francs his father gave him every month. By now (1832) the arrangement has lasted ten years. Unfortunately, Barral has lately become a rich man, having inherited a fortune that brings him an income of 20,000 francs a year, and with his wealth he has turned into a frightful miser.

I myself had been very much in love with Annette for two weeks, but after that I found her ideas *narrow and Parisian*. For me that is the best antidote for love. And when of an evening I met my boyhood friend and his good Annette strolling along the dusty Boulevard de Gand, I would have nothing to say to them. I was perishing of boredom and grief; not even the harlots could cheer me up.

At last, toward half-past ten, I could go to Mme. Pasta's to play faro. It always vexed me to be the first-comer and to be forced to carry on a conversation, all on the level of kitchen gossip, with Rachel, Giuditta Pasta's mother. But at any rate she spoke Italian to me, and sometimes I found her with some idiot just arrived from Milan, to whom she had just given a meal.

With great caution I would sound out these blockheads on all the pretty women in Milan. I would have died rather than mention the name of Metilda, but sometimes they spoke of her of their own accord. Such evenings were great events in my life. Then when the others came in we would begin to play faro.

Deep in reverie, I would win or lose thirty francs in the course of four hours. I was so lax in regard to these debts of honor that when I lost more than I had in my pocket I would say to whoever won: "Shall I go up to my room for the money?" To which he would reply: *"Non, si figuri!"*[17]

And I would put off paying him until the next day. I did this so often that I came to be known as a pauper. Later on I realized my mistake because of the lamentations of the excellent Pasta, Judith's husband, whenever he saw me lose thirty francs or so. But even after my eyes were opened on this point, I did not alter my behavior.

CHAPTER VI

OCCASIONALLY WHEN I BOUGHT A BOOK I WOULD WRITE IN it the date of purchase and a note on the feelings dominating me at the moment. Perhaps I may be able to find some of the dates of events in this period among my books.[1]

Thus I am not certain how I got the idea of going to England. When I wrote to M. . . . , my banker, to give me a letter of credit for a thousand crowns on London, he replied that all he had left for me was one hundred and twenty-six francs. But I must have had money elsewhere, perhaps at Grenoble. I had it sent to me and set off on my travels.[2]

My first impressions of London therefore were formed in 1821. One day in Milan, around 1816, as I remember, I was discussing the subject of suicide with the celebrated Brougham (Lord Brougham, now Lord High Chancellor of England, who will probably die soon of overwork).

"What could be more disagreeable," M. Brougham said to me, "than the thought that all the newspapers, on announcing that you had blown your brains out, would go prying into your private life to discover the motives for your act? . . . It's enough to take away one's appetite for suicide."

"But what could be simpler," I answered, "than to form the habit of going out in a fishing boat? One day when the sea was rough you could fall overboard by accident."

The idea of taking a sea voyage was indeed very attractive to me. Besides, the only writer I found readable was Shakespeare, and I looked forward with the greatest pleasure to seeing his works performed on the stage. During my first trip to England in 1817 I had not seen any of Shakespeare's plays produced.

In all my life I have loved only three men passionately: Cimarosa, Mozart and Shakespeare. In 1820, when I was in Milan, I seriously considered having that statement engraved on my tombstone. For days I pondered over the wording, certain that I would never find peace except in the grave. I decided on a marble tablet in the form of a playing card, with the inscription:

ERRICO BEYLE
MILANESE
Visse, scrisse, amó
Quest' anima
Adorava
Cimarosa, Mozart e Shakespeare
Mori de anni . . . .
il . . . 18 . . .[3]

No foul insignia to be added, no insipid ornament; the inscription to be carved in capital letters. I despise Grenoble,[4] but ever since I arrived in Milan for the first time in May 1800 I have loved that city.

There I knew the greatest happiness and the greatest pain; there above all I had my first experience of pleasure, which makes a place home. There I desire to spend my old age and there I hope to die.

How often, when sailing over the waves of Lake Como in a solitary boat, have I said to myself exultantly:

Hic captabis frigus opacum![5]

If I leave enough money to set up this tablet, I beg that it be placed over my body in the cemetery at Andilly, near Montmorency, facing the east. I particularly do not wish to have any other monument, nothing in the Parisian style, no *cheap theatrics* of the type I abhor. In 1821 I found that sort of vaudeville even more detestable. The French mentality in the Paris theatres almost made me cry aloud: "Scoundrels! Scoundrels! Scoundrels!" And I would rush away after the first act. But when French music was added to the French spirit, my *disgust* reached such a pitch that I would grimace and make a spectacle of myself. One day Mme. de Longueville offered me her box at the Feydeau Theatre. By good luck I went alone, but after fifteen minutes I fled, making horrible faces and vowing not to enter the Feydeau Theatre for two years, a pledge I kept faithfully.

Anything that savored of the novels of Mme. de Genlis, or the poetry of Legouve, Louy, Campenon or Treneuil had the same effect on me.

To say this in 1832 sounds very flat, since everyone agrees with me now. But in 1821, Lussinge used to mock at what he considered my unbearable arrogance whenever I disclosed this violent revulsion in his hearing. No doubt he surmised that M. de Jouy or M. Campenon had aroused my enmity by writing a savage criticism of one of my books. But a critic who jeers at me excites a totally different reaction in my mind. Every time I reread his criticism I make another effort to decide who is right, he or I.

It was in September 1821, as I recall, that I set out for London. I felt nothing but loathing for Paris at the time. Had I not been so blind, I should have sought the advice of Countess de Tracy on my problems, even though she was then sixty-three years old. I loved that adorable woman like a mother, nay, like a woman who had once been beautiful, but without a trace of earthly love. However, I had repelled her friendship through my too great reserve. I should have tried to be the friend, not the lover, of Céline. I don't know whether I should have succeeded in becoming her lover, but I see clearly today that I was on the brink of becoming her intimate friend. Neither should I have refused to renew my acquaintance with the Countess Berthois.

I was in despair, or to put it more accurately, I was disgusted with life in Paris, and with myself above all. I had every fault in the calendar, so far as I could judge; I wished I were someone else. I went to London then to find a cure for my spleen, and to a certain degree I found it. What I needed most was to put up an obstruction between me and the Milan cathedral. The plays of Shakespeare and the acting of Kean provided this obstruction.

Not infrequently people would come up to me at some social gathering and compliment me on one of my books; at that time I had written only a few. But once the compliment was paid and acknowledged, we had nothing more to say to one another. Those Parisian flatterers, expecting more cheap theatrics in my reply, must have found me a very awkward fellow, or perhaps thought I was puffed up. But I am accustomed to appearing the opposite of what I really am. I have always looked on my books as if they were lottery tickets. All I care about is to be reprinted in 1900. Petrarch however counted on his Latin poem *Africa* to bring him fame, never dreaming that he would be known for his sonnets.

Among those who paid me compliments of this sort were two men whose approval was very flattering to me. One, a man of fifty, tall, and extremely handsome, was the very image of *Jupiter Mansuetus.* In 1821 I was still under the spell of the emotions that had led me to begin the second volume of my *Histoire de la Peinture* four years earlier. But my handsome admirer spoke in the affected style of Voltaire's letters. He had once been condemned to death in Naples, either in 1799 or 1800. His name was di Fiori,[6] and today he is one of my dearest friends. Ten years passed before we began to understand each other, for at first I did not know how to respond to his Voltairean hyperboles.

My second admirer was *Edouard Edwards,* a man of about thirty, with a magnificent head of flaxen ringlets, characteristically English. In London, years before, he had been a ne'er-do-well, always down at the heels, but later he had served in the quartermaster corps of Wellington's army of occupation. Having learned of his earlier career as a newspaper hack, bent on winning fame by getting off some resounding pun, I was greatly astonished to discover on longer acquaintance that he was not a swindler. Poor Edouard Edwards had one redeeming trait: he was by nature absolutely fearless. Courage was so instinctive with him that although he boasted about everything else with a vanity exceeding that of the French, if that is possible, and without any French reserve, moreover, he never mentioned his own valor.

I ran into M. Edouard in the Calais coach. Finding himself in the company of a French author, he felt obliged to make conversation, which was a stroke of luck for me. I had counted on the landscape for diversion, but there is nothing so dull (for me at least) as the drive through Abbéville, Montreuil-sur-Mer, etc. Without Edwards' chatter, those long white roads running across the slightly undulating countryside would have been a sore trial.

However, the walls of Montreuil and the chinaware at lunch gave me a foretaste of England.

We had a traveling companion in a man named *Smidt*,[7] former secretary to M. Fréville, Councillor of State, and one of the pettiest schemers in the world.

I had met M. Fréville at Mme. Nardot's house, at 4 rue des Menars. Poor Smidt, who had started out in life as a fairly honest fellow, had ended up as a political spy. M. Decazes[8] used to send him to Aix-la-Chapelle to spy on conferences of ambassadors who were taking the waters there.

He was always a schemer, and in the end, if I am not mistaken, he became a very shifty fellow, changing his address every six months. One day Smidt told me that he was going to marry the daughter of Marshal Oudinot, Duke of Reggio, not for love, but for money. Now as a matter of fact Marshal Oudinot had a regiment of daughters, and used to go abegging to Louis XVIII every six months.

Surprised by this announcement, I said to Smidt: "Marry her tonight, old man."

But two weeks later I learned that the Duke Decazes unfortunately had learned of the true state of poor Smidt's fortunes, and felt obliged to write a word of warning to the prospective father-in-law. All the same Smidt was a good enough chap and pleasant company.

At Calais I did something very stupid. We dined in the common room at the inn, where I drank so much English ale that I must have been a bit tipsy. At any rate I was very gay, babbling on like a man who had been tongue-tied for a year. There was a boor at our table, an English captain in the coasting trade, who seemed to take exception to some of my stories, but I took no offence, answering him good-naturedly. That night, for the first time in my life, I had a frightful case of indigestion. Several days later *Edwards,* in measured tones quite unusual for him, told me that I should have given the captain at Calais a good dressing-down instead of taking his remarks so lightly.

I had made a similar blunder once before, at Dresden in 1813, with regard to M . . . , who has since gone mad. I am not at all lacking in courage; a thing like that could not happen to me today. But in my youth, when I gave free rein to my tongue, I ran wild, all intent as I was on the beauty of the images I was trying to communicate. Edwards' admonition had the same effect on me as the crowing of the cock on Saint Peter. We spent two days looking for that English captain in all the low taverns frequented by seafaring men near the Tower, as I recall.

It was on the second day of our search, I believe, that Edwards said to me soberly and politely, with even a touch of courtliness in his manner, "Every nation, you know, has its own code in fighting a duel. We English are more or less whimsical in this matter, etc., etc."

The point of all this philosophizing was that he wanted me to let him speak for me to the captain, who, despite the antagonism of all Englishmen for the French, would probably claim that he had had no intention of insulting me. Edwards was willing to bet ten to one on this. At any rate, if it came to a duel, Edwards entreated me to let him fight in my place. "Are you trying to make game of me?" I exclaimed with an oath.

We exchanged a few hot words, but in the end he convinced me that he had merely been somewhat overzealous, and we resumed our search for the captain. Once or twice my hair stood on end when I thought I had recognized him. Since then I have realized that the affair would have been quite difficult for me without Edwards. I had been drunk with high spirits, with talk and with ale at Calais. This was my first infidelity to the memory of Milan.

I found London quite touching, especially during my walks along the Thames toward *Little Chelsea* (little chelsy). The small rose-covered cottages there struck me as truly elegiac. It was the first time that this sentimental style of architecture ever appealed to me.*

Nowadays I realize that I have always had a morbid disposition. I used to feel a revulsion, almost the rage of hydrophobia, in the presence of gross people. The talk of a fat, vulgar merchant from the provinces used to have a stupefying effect on me, and would leave me miserable for the rest of the day. Charles Durand, the rich banker of Grenoble, for example, affected me that way, although his attitude toward me was very friendly. This disposition, which dates back to my childhood, and gave me so many bad moments between the ages of fifteen and twenty-five, grew stronger in later years. It made me so unhappy that I could bear none but familiar faces about me. Any strange face, which, had I been in a healthy state, would have diverted me, got on my nerves at such times.

---

* In five days, from the 20th to the 24th of June, I have reached this point, *id est*, the 148th page. Rome, June 1832.

Yesterday I received a letter from Kashmir, dated June 1831, from Victor Jacquemont.—Beyle.

By chance I put up at the Tavistock Hotel in Covent Garden, a hotel frequented by well-to-do provincials on a visit to London. My room, which I always left unlocked with impunity, though thieving is common in that country, was no more than eight feet wide and ten feet long. In compensation for this, the dining room was probably a hundred feet long, thirty feet wide, and twenty feet high. You could eat whatever and as much as you desired for only fifty sous (two shillings). They served us innumerable beefsteaks, or placed a huge forty-pound roast of beef on the table, with a sharp carving knife for us to take as much as we liked. Then came the hot tea in which all this meat was to be cooked in the stomach. The dining room opened on an arcade that gave on Covent Garden. Every morning I would see some thirty solid Britishers there, walking gravely to and fro, many of them with a somber air. They betrayed none of the affectation, none of the shrill frivolity of the French. This suited my mood, and made me less unhappy. I cannot say that the hours I spent in that dining room were merry, but they were to my liking.

JUNE 25.

I learned to read the English newspapers mechanically, although at bottom they did not interest me in the least. Later on, in 1826, I had a wretched time at another hotel on Covent Garden Place called the Ouakum, or some such awkward name, on the corner opposite the Tavistock. But from 1826 to 1832 I had no particular misfortunes.

There was no play of Shakespeare's being performed the day of my arrival in London in 1821; I went instead to the Haymarket Theatre, which, as I remember, was open. In spite of the drab look of the interior, I rather enjoyed myself.

The play given was *She Stoops to Conquer,* a comedy by [Goldsmith] which I found extremely diverting because of the comical grimaces of the actor who played the husband Miss [Hardcastle] was trying to conquer by lowering herself. The subject is somewhat the same as in Marivaux's play *[Fausses Confidences].* A girl disguises herself as a chambermaid in order to win the man she wants to marry, a clever stratagem, I find, and highly entertaining.

During the day I used to wander about the environs of London, often going as far as Richmond.

The famous terrace at Richmond looks out on rolling country like the view from Saint-Germain-en-Laye, except that here the escarpment is not quite so high, and the eye falls on fields of rich green studded with huge trees of venerable age, while from the terrace at Saint-Germain, one sees only a dry and stony landscape. The fresh green of the English country-side and the beauty of its trees are unique; in fact, it is considered dishonorable and criminal to cut down a tree in England, while a French landowner thinks nothing of selling the five or six great oaks on his estate the moment he needs some ready cash. The view from Richmond, and that from Windsor too, remind me of my beloved Lombardy, the mountains of Brianza, Desio, Como, Cadenabbia, the Sacro Monte and Varese, all those beautiful regions associated in my mind with my happiest hours.

I was so distraught in those moments of happiness that I have retained almost no distinct memories of them; at most there is some date marked in a book I was reading, with a note of the place where I happened to be at the time. Whenever I reread such a book, the slightest notation in the margin enables me to pick up the thread of my recollections and *proceed from there.* But if on reading a book over I find no such notes, I must start all over again from the beginning.

One afternoon I was seated on the bridge below the terrace at Richmond, reading one of my favorite books, the *Memoirs of Mrs. Hutchinson,* when a man stopped in front of me and exclaimed:

"Mister Bell!"

It was B . . . , whom I had met in Milan at the home of Lady Jersey. He was a man of great refinement, some fifty years old, who, though not quite a member of the upper classes, was admitted to their society. (In England the classes are as sharply divided as in India, the land of the pariahs; see *La Chaumière Indienne?*)[9]

"Have you been to see Lady Jersey?"

"No, I did not know her well enough in Milan, and people say that you English travelers are inclined to forget your acquaintances when you come back across the Channel."

"What a strange notion! Go to see her."

"It would give me far more pain to be received coldly, or not to be recognized, than it would gratify me to receive the warmest welcome."

"Then you haven't seen Mr. Hobhouse, or Mr. Brougham either?"

I gave the same reply.

Mr. B . . . , who was as nimble as a diplomat, then asked me many questions about France. I told him that the young men of the lower middle classes, well-educated but unable to get on in the world, seeing that the hirelings of the Congregation stood in their way, would one day overturn the Congregation and the Bourbons as well, when the chance came. (Since this sounds like a correct prediction, I accord the kind reader full right not to believe that I made it.)

I inserted that sentence to show that my great disgust for the situation I was describing in France gave me that look of discontent without which one is not esteemed in England.

When Mr. B . . . realized that I was acquainted with M. de Lafayette and M. de Tracy, he exclaimed in the greatest astonishment: "*You didn't set your sights high enough on this trip!* You needed only to have said the word, and you could have dined twice a week at Lord Holland's, at Lady A . . . 's or Lady . . ."

"But I never even mentioned to my friends in Paris that I was going to London. My sole reason for coming was to see the plays of Shakespeare performed on the stage."

When B . . . finally grasped what I was saying, he thought I had gone out of my mind.

The first time I went to Almack's ball, my banker, on seeing my ticket of admission, said to me with a sigh:

"For twenty-two years, sir, I have been trying my best to get a ticket to that ball, which you will attend in an hour from now."

Since English society is divided by rings like those on a bamboo stick, the greatest preoccupation of every man here is to climb into the class above his own, while the members of that class do everything possible to push him down.

At only one period did I observe such practices in France, and that was when the former generals in Napoleon's army resorted to the lowest tricks to gain admission to the salon of Mme. Talaru and others in the Faubourg Saint-Germain. The toads these vile fellows had to swallow every day would fill fifty pages. Poor Amédée de Pastoret would have some fine stories to tell if ever he wrote his memoirs.[10]

Ah well, I don't believe that the young men who are preparing for the bar now in 1832 have it in them to put up with such humiliations. They may be capable of base actions, even acts of villainy, if you will, but to submit like those generals I have described to being slain by pinpricks, the pinpricks of contempt, would be altogether unnatural for anyone who was not brought up in the salons of 1780, as they were resuscitated between 1804 and 1830.

Abject characters of this kind, who bear with anything at the hands of a *cordon bleu*[11] (Mme. Talaru) will not be found in the future except among young men born in Paris.

And Louis-Philippe enjoys too little prestige for such salons to be revived in Paris for a long time.

The Reform Bill (June 1832) just passed in England will probably halt the production of men like Mr. B . . . , who could not forgive me for not *setting my sights high enough* on my trip. In 1821 I did not realize how far this type of degradation could go, as I did later on, when I returned to England in 1826. The dinners and balls of the aristocracy cost a mint of money, and it is money prodigiously ill-spent.

I am obliged to B . . . for one thing; he showed me how to return to London from Richmond by water, a delightful voyage.

At last, on the . . . of June, a performance of *Othello,* with Kean in the title role, was announced. I was nearly trampled to death before I could get my ticket to the pit. While waiting in the queue I was reminded of the great days of my youth, in 1800, when we struggled through a similar mob to see the first performance of *Pinto*[12] (Germinal, year VIII).

The poor wretch who wants to buy a ticket for the pit at Covent Garden is trapped in a winding passage three feet wide, lined with wooden panels that have been rubbed smooth by the clothing of his fellow-victims.

My head was so crammed with literary ideas that it was not until I had entered that gloomy passageway, when my anger had given me enough strength to push my way through the crowd, that I said to myself: "How stupid of me not to have bought a ticket for a box in advance! I will not be able to enjoy the play tonight!"

Fortunately, when I reached my seat in the pit, the very people who had been shouldering me in the corridor seemed to regard me with a frank and kindly eye. We exchanged a few pleasantries on our recent troubles, and as my anger subsided, I gave myself over to admiring Kean, with whom I was acquainted only through the hyperboles of my traveling companion, Edouard Edwards. It seems that Kean is a low fellow, a hero of the public houses.

For this I found it easy to forgive him; had he been born rich or of a good family he would not have been Kean, but a coxcomb, without a spark of life. The good manners of the upper classes in France, and no doubt in England, too, *condemn any show of energy*, which is to be indulged in only as if by some accident. When M. de Syon or some other young man from the Faubourg Saint-Germain is announced at M. de Tracy's, I expect to see a person of exquisite breeding and absolutely no energy. And yet in 1821 I was not in a position to judge the degree of triviality these colorless creatures represented. M. de Syon, who is a friend of General Lafayette, and went to America in his train, I believe, must seem to be bursting with energy in the salon of Mme. de Trémoille, compared with her other guests![13]

Heavens! How can men possibly be so trivial! And how can one describe such people! I used to ponder over this in the winter of 1830, when I was making a study of these gilded youths. At that period their greatest concern was to make sure that their hair, dressed according to the latest fashion, in a roll across the forehead, should not fall down over their eyes.*

My pleasure in seeing Kean was mingled with no little surprise. The English, a hot-tempered people, use gestures quite different from ours to express the same emotions.

Baron Lussinge and the excellent Barot came over to join me in London; perhaps Lussinge accompanied me there.

I have an unfortunate talent for communicating my tastes to others; often, when speaking of my mistresses to my friends, I would cause my friends to fall in love with them, or, what is worse, I made my mistress fall in love with the friend whom I really loved. This is what happened in the case of Mme. Azur and Mérimée. For four days I was in despair. When I felt a little better I went to Mérimée and begged him to grant me two weeks of grace. "Two years, if you wish," he replied. "She is not to my taste. She wears her stockings wrinkled on her leg" (*en garaude,* as they say in Grenoble).

Barot, who always does things deliberately, like a business man, engaged a valet for us. He was a little English fop, of the type I despise most. For them fashion is not a pleasure, but a serious duty, not to be neglected at any cost. Since I am a sensible man about everything but certain memories of the past, I quickly grasped the absurdity of the forty-eight hours of toil imposed on the English workingman. A poor Italian, dressed in rags, is far happier. He has time to make love, and he devotes between eight and a hundred days a year to the observance of a religion which is all the more amusing because it instills fear in him, etc.

---

* *For me:* I am somewhat discouraged by my complete forgetfulness of dates. The imagination is stifled by running after dates instead of trying to remember facts.—*Beyle.*

My companions made no end of fun of me for entertaining such opinions. And yet my supposed paradox is fast coming to be recognized as the truth, and will be a commonplace by 1840. My friends also called me a fool when I added that the excessive and crushing labor of the English workman was our revenge for Waterloo and the four coalitions. We at least have buried our dead, and those of us who survive are better off than the English. But as long as they live Barot and Lussinge will regard me as a stubborn fellow. Even now, ten years later, when I try to shame them by saying: "You see, today you hold the same opinions that I did in London in 1821," they deny it, and my reputation for obstinacy persists. Imagine what I suffered whenever I had the ill-luck to talk to these men about literature. My cousin Colomb for a long time thought I was really consumed by jealousy because I told him that M. Villemain's *Lascaris* was as dull as ditchwater. And great God, what a clamor they made when I broached general principles!

One day when I was speaking of the great labors of the English, our smug little valet protested that the honor of his country was impugned.

"Quite right," I said to him, "but you must understand that we are in an unfortunate position; we don't know any amusing people here."

"Sir, I will see to that for you," he answered. "I will make all the arrangements. Don't apply to anyone else; they will make you pay through the nose, etc."

My friends laughed. Thus as a result of poking fun at the valet's honor, I was lured into an affair with some wenches. Nothing could have been more disagreeable, more repulsive, in fact, than the way in which our man, while directing us about

London the next day, made us listen to all the details of the bargain he had struck.

In the first place, the girls lived in a lonely quarter of town, out on Westminster Road, the kind of place where Frenchmen might well expect to be set upon by a gang of sailors or pimps. When we mentioned the matter to an English friend, he said: "Watch out for an ambuscade!"

Our valet told us that he had haggled a long time to obtain the privilege of having tea served to us in the morning when we got up. At first the girls refused to grant us their favors and tea as well for only twenty-one shillings (twenty-five francs and five sous) but at last they had consented. Several Englishmen tried to warn us:

"An Englishman would never fall into such a trap. Do you realize that you will be several miles out of London?"

It was agreed among us that we would not go. But when the appointed evening came, Barot looked at me inquiringly. I knew what he meant.

"We are strong," I said, "and we have arms."

Lussinge dared not come with us.

We took a cab, Barot and I. The road led across Westminster Bridge, and then through streets without dwellings, shut in between garden walls.

Barot laughed.

"Considering how brilliantly you conducted yourself with Alexandrine, in an elegant establishment, in the middle of Paris, what do you expect to accomplish here?"

I was indeed very depressed. If not for the dullness of London after the dinner hour, especially when the theatres were closed, as happened that day, and if not for the slight element of danger in the affair, Westminster Road would never have seen me. After almost going off the road several times into unpaved lanes, the driver, swearing all the while, finally pulled up in front of a three-story house that altogether was no more than twenty-five feet high. I have never seen such a tiny house in all my life.

Certainly without the thought of possible danger I would never have entered that house. I expected to find three vicious trollops, but instead we were met by three shy little girls, very pale and eager to please, with beautiful chestnut hair.

The furniture was absurdly tiny. Since Barot is tall and portly, and I too am stout, we literally could not find a seat. It was like being in a doll's house, and we were afraid we might crash through the chairs. When the little girls saw our distress, their own increased. Happily Barot was inspired to mention the garden.

"Oh yes, we have a garden," they said, not with pride, but as if delighted to show us something a bit more luxurious. We went down into the garden, carrying candles to light the way. It was all of twenty-five feet long and ten feet wide. Barot and I burst into laughter. All the domestic utensils of the poor were there: a little wash-tub, a little vat with a spiral device for brewing beer.

I was touched, but Barot was so disgusted that he said to me in French: "Let's pay them off and clear out."

"But they will be so humiliated," I replied.

"Bah! Humiliated! Little do you know them! If it's not too late, they will simply send for other customers, or for their lovers, if this is anything like France."

These sound observations made no impression on me. The girls' obvious poverty, their toy furniture, so old and yet so clean, had touched my heart. Before we had finished drinking our tea I was on such intimate terms with them that, in my broken English, I confessed our earlier fears of being murdered. This disconcerted them completely.

"But after all," I added, "the proof that we trust you is that I am telling you all this."

We sent our valet away. And then I felt as if I were with warm friends from whom I had been parted for long years.

Not a door in the house could be closed properly, another cause for suspicion when we went to bed. But what was the use of having doors and strong locks, when any of the partitions would have crumbled under a blow? You could hear whatever was said all over the house. Barot, who had gone up to the third floor, shouted to me:

"If anyone tries to murder you, call me!"

I wanted to keep the light on, but my modest little friend, otherwise so gentle and submissive, would not allow it. When she saw me lay out my pistols and dagger on the night table beside the bed, facing the door, she gave a great start of fear. She was charming, small, pale, but well-formed.

No one murdered us. The next day we dispensed with their tea and sent the valet to fetch Lussinge, telling him to bring cold meat and wine. In a short time he drove up with an excellent lunch in tow, quite astonished at our enthusiasm.

JUNE 26.

The two sisters sent for one of their friends. We left them some wine and cold meat, of finer quality, apparently, than any they had ever seen.

When we told them that we would return, they thought we were making fun of them. Miss . . . , my little friend, took me aside and said:

"If I were sure you would return this evening, I would not go out. But I suppose our house is too shabby for men like you."

All day long I looked forward to the pleasant evening that awaited me with my gentle, quiet friends (*full of snugness*)[14].

The play that afternoon seemed long drawn-out. Barot and Lussinge wanted to have a good look at all the shameless hussies who crowded into the lobby of Covent Garden. At last Barot and I set out for our little cottage, where the poor girls opened their eyes wide when they saw us unwrap bottles of claret and champagne. I have a notion that they had never before been confronted with a bottle of *real champaign*[15] that had not already been broached.

Fortunately the corks of our bottles popped in the approved manner, thereby rendering their happiness complete. Their transports were, however, quiet and decorous. In fact their whole behavior was marked by extreme decorum.—But we already knew this.

The amusing thing is that during my entire stay in England I was always unhappy unless I could finish the day with a visit to that little house.

This relationship was the first real consolation I found for the misery that was poisoning my hours of solitude. It is apparent that I was no more than twenty years old in 1821. If I had been thirty-eight, as my baptismal certificate would seem to indicate, I could have tried to find similar consolation among the respectable women of Paris who had shown some sympathy for me. Sometimes, however, I doubt that I would have succeeded there. What goes by the name of the highest breeding, an air that supposedly distinguishes the manners of Mme. de Marmier from those of Mme. Edwards, often strikes me as damnable affectation, and at once seals my heart hermetically.

This is one of my great afflictions. Does the reader share my sensibility in this regard? I am always mortally offended by the slightest nuances in behavior.

When I see the grand airs displayed in high society I cry out inwardly: *Bourgeoise!* or *Puppet of the Boulevard Saint-Germain!* and I promptly turn disagreeable and ironical to the next person I meet.

One can understand everything except oneself, to which one of those polished products from the aristocratic quarter of Paris would add, in order to avoid any possibility of ridicule: "I am far from believing that I understand everything." My doctors always enjoy treating me when I am ill, because they consider me a rare example of *nervous irritability*. On one occasion I caught a chill from an open window in the next room, whose door was closed. The slightest odor (except bad ones) takes all the strength put of my left arm and leg, and tends to make me fall over on that side.

"But what detestable egotism you show by mentioning all these details!"

"To be sure, and what is this book if not a work of detestable egotism! And what good would it do to display the grace of a pedant in a book of this kind, like M. Villemain in yesterday's article on the arrest of M. de Chateaubriand?"

If this book of mine is tedious, two years after publication it will be used to wrap up parcels of butter at the grocer's; if it is not tedious, it will prove that egotism, that is, *sincere egotism,* is one way of describing the human heart, in the knowledge of which we have made giant strides since 1721, when Montesquieu, that great man whom I have studied so faithfully, wrote *Les Lettres Persanes.*

The progress we have made since that period is so amazing that sometimes Montesquieu seems crude in comparison.*

After I began spending my evenings in this homely fashion, I felt so much at ease in London despite my poor command of English that I let my friends go back to Paris without me. Lussinge had to return to his office, and Barot to his business affairs of baccarat and carding machines.[16]

I must admit that their company had been very agreeable to me, perhaps because we avoided discussing the fine arts, a subject that has always been a stumbling block between me and my friends.

The British, I believe, are the most obtuse, the most barbarous people in the world. So much so that I forgive them for their infamous actions at Saint-Helena. They were unaware of the barbarity of their conduct. Of course an Italian, or even a German, on seeing Napoleon's sufferings at Saint-Helena, would have had some conception of the great man's martyrdom. But these respectable English, haunted by the dread of starving to death if they stop working for an instant, and conscious only of *skirting* the dangerous abyss of want, these respectable Englishmen, I say, put the thought of Saint-Helena out of mind just as they dismiss the thought of Raphael. These are subjects that might make them *lose time,* and that's all.

---

* I am happy to be writing this. My official duties have kept me busy on one thing or another night and day for three days (June 1832). In any case I would have been unable to continue my confidential memorandum to the Minister at four o'clock—a work of imagination. But I do this easily, with no more trouble or plan than is involved in simply remembering.—*Beyle.*

Stendhal wrote confidential diplomatic reports for Count Sebastiani, Minister of Foreign Affairs in Paris, and for Count Molé, and Guizot, from 1831 to 1834.—*Ed.*

The three of us together made up one fairly well-rounded traveler: I for my daydreams and my knowledge of Say and Smith (Adam); Baron Lussinge for his ability to see the bad side of everything; and Barot for his practical spirit (knowing how to exchange one pound of steel, worth twelve francs, for three-quarters of a pound of watch-springs, worth 10,000 francs).

Once I was alone I vacillated between respect for the decency of the average British family with an income of 10,000 francs a year, and scorn for the complete demoralization of the Englishman with expensive tastes who realizes that in order to satisfy them he must sell out to the government. The vilest and most absurd[17] person you can listen to in the whole world is an English Philippe de Ségur.

Because I was unable to resolve the conflict in my mind on this point, I departed without being able to decide whether or not the English would need a *Terror* to clean out their Augean Stables.

The poor lass with whom I spent my evenings pleaded with me to take her to France, assuring me that she would live on potatoes and be no charge to me.

But I had once been severely punished for having invited a sister of mine to join me in Milan, in 1816, as I recall. Mme. Périer clung to me like a leech, burdening me day and night with the responsibility for what was to become of her. My sister, to be sure, had every virtue, and was fairly reasonable and amiable besides. But I was obliged to quarrel with her to rid myself of the barnacle that had attached itself to the keel of my vessel, and against my will made me responsible for all her future happiness. A terrible situation it was!

It was the thought of her that prevented me from taking Miss Appleby to Paris with me.

And yet if I had done so, I should have been spared many an hour of fiendish gloom. It was my unhappy fate to find affectation so repugnant that it was very hard for me to be simple, sincere, kind, in a word, perfectly "German" with a French woman.

(I shall fill out this section on London when I can lay my hands on my copies of the English plays with notes of the dates when I saw them performed.)

The day before I left it was announced that eight poor devils were to be publicly hanged. In my view, the hanging of a thief or a murderer in England means that the aristocracy is sacrificing a victim to its security, for it is the aristocracy that drives men to be miscreants. This truth, that seems so paradoxical today, may be a commonplace when my scribblings are finally read.

I spent the night before the hanging telling myself that it was the duty of the traveler to see such spectacles and the effect they produced on the native population (*who has raciness*)[18].

But the next day, when the servant came to wake me at eight o'clock, it was raining in torrents. The thing I was trying to force myself to do seemed so painful that I still remember my inward struggle. I did not go to see that barbarous spectacle.

Chapter VII

On my return to paris, around the month of December, I found myself taking a little more interest in men and things. Today I realize that this was because I had learned that regardless of what I had left behind in Milan, I could still enjoy a modicum of happiness, or at least some diversion, elsewhere. This "elsewhere" was the little cottage of Miss Appleby.

But I did not have enough good sense to arrange my life systematically. My friendships were always a matter of accident. For example:

There once was a minister of war in Naples whose name was Micheroux, a penniless soldier of fortune who came originally, I believe, from Liège. When he died, all he could bequeath to his two sons was a pension from the court. In Naples one relies on the bounty of the king as on a promised legacy.

One of these sons, the Chevalier Alexandre Micheroux, used to dine with us at the Hotel de Bruxelles at 47 rue de Richelieu. He was a handsome fellow with the phlegmatic appearance of a Dutchman, but he had fallen on evil days. When the revolution broke out in 1820, he was living quietly in Naples, under the special protection of Crown Prince Francesco, then acting as regent but later known as the most contemptible of kings.

One day Francesco summoned Micheroux to him, and addressing him with the familiar "thou," begged him to accept the post of Minister to Dresden. A lackadaisical fellow, Micheroux felt no interest in the appointment, but as he lacked the courage to oppose a royal highness and a hereditary prince, he went to Dresden. He was gone only a short time when Francesco issued a decree banishing him from Naples, following this with a sentence of death in absentia, if I remember rightly, or at any rate the confiscation of his annuity.

Though he had no special gifts or aptitudes, the Chevalier had always been his own stern taskmaster. For many years he toiled eighteen hours a day, just like an Englishman, to become a painter, a musician, a metaphysician, what not? He persevered in these studies in defiance of all reason.

I happened to hear of his astonishing labors through an actress of my acquaintance, who from her window used to see this handsome young man standing at his easel from five in the morning until five in the afternoon, after which he spent the rest of the evening reading. As a result of all this fearful toil in the arts, the Chevalier wound up, at any rate, with the ability to play a first-rate accompaniment on the piano, and with enough common sense or musical taste, whichever you please, not to be taken in by the froth and fanfaronade of Rossini. However, as soon as he tried to reason about anything, his feeble brain, stuffed with false knowledge, lapsed at once into the most comical blunders. He was particularly unreliable in any discussion of politics. I have never known anyone more lyrical and absurd than the Italian *carbonari* who filled the liberal salons of Paris during the 1820s.

One evening Micheroux left us after dinner and went up to his room. Two hours later we noticed that he had not come to the Café de Foy, when one of us was paying for a round of coffee, and on going up to look for him, we found that he had fainted dead away. He had gonorrhea, and on this particular evening the pain had become excessive right after dinner. In his phlegmatic way the poor fellow had begun to reckon up his troubles, including his desperate need of money, until the pain had overwhelmed him. Another man would have killed himself in the same situation, but Micheroux would have been satisfied to die in a swoon if we had not gone to some trouble to bring him around.

The man touched me, perhaps because I realized that here was a human being even more unhappy than I. Barot lent him five hundred francs, which he returned later. The next day either Lussinge or I introduced him to Mme. Pasta.

A week later we realized that he had become her favorite. And yet no two people were ever cooler and more reasonable in their attitude toward each other. After observing them every day for four or five years, it would not have surprised me, if by some magic spell I could have been present and invisible when they were alone together, to discover that they never made love, but passed the time talking about music. I am sure that although she lived in Paris for eight or ten years, and for most of that time was extremely popular, Mme. Pasta never had a French lover.*

JUNE 30, 1832.

At about the same time that we presented Micheroux to Mme. Pasta, the handsome General Lagrange also made his appearance in her drawing-room, where he sat beside her on

---

* June 30, 1832. Twelve pages *written* late in the evening, after having finished my official duties. I should not have worked so well at a book of imagination.—*Beyle.*

the sofa and wearied us all with his talk the whole evening long. It was he who used to dress up as Apollo or "the Spanish slave" at the costume balls of the Imperial Court. Once I saw Queen Caroline Murat and the divine Princess Borghese, clad in Indian costume, dancing with him at one of those balls. He is beyond question one of the most empty-headed men to be found in good society, which is saying a great deal.

Should the men of the future be less shallow than my contemporaries, as is probable, they will be able to judge how insipid our good society was when I say here that it was much more disastrous for a young blood of our time to fall into some impropriety of expression than it was profitable for him to make some bright remark.

The Chevalier Micheroux had distinguished, almost exquisite manners. In this regard he was quite the opposite of Lussinge, and of Barot too, who, though he happened to have made millions, was only a bluff and hearty fellow from the provinces. Micheroux's elegant manners attracted me, but I soon perceived that he was essentially a cold man.

He had studied music the way a savant of the Academy of Inscriptions studies, or pretends to study Persian. He had *learned* to admire such and such a piece of music, and for him the finest qualities in a composition were strict harmony and correct phrasing.

In my view the finest quality, by far, is to be *expressive*.

As far as I am concerned the finest quality in any of the arts, in everything that is black on white, is to be able to say with Boileau:

> *Et mon vers, bien ou mal, dit toujours quelque chose.*[1]

It was after the attachment between Micheroux and Mme. Pasta was established on a permanent basis that I moved over to the Hotel de Lillois, taking a room on the fourth floor. At first her suite comprised the whole third floor, but later she moved to the second.

Mme. Pasta had no faults or vices that I could see; she was artless, even-tempered, just, and natural, and moreover she had the greatest talent for the acting of tragedy that I have ever known.

As is customary with young men (it must be remembered that I was only "twenty" in 1821) at first I longed to have her fall in love with me, since I admired her so much. Today I realize that she was too cold and rational, not wanton or caressing enough for our affair to have lasted, if we had ever come to that. For me it could only have been a passing fancy, and she, justifiably indignant, would have broken with me permanently. It was better, therefore, that our relations were limited to the most chaste and devoted friendship on my part, and on hers to much the same feeling, though with some ups and downs.

Micheroux, fearing me a little, told her a few slanderous tales about me, the effect of which I *blunted* by simply paying no attention to them. After six months or so, Mme. Pasta must have said to herself that there was nothing in it.

But such talk always leaves some residue, and the result was that after six or eight years our relations became quite cool. I never felt the slightest resentment towards Micheroux. After having been so royally mistreated by King Francesco, he could say, like one of Voltaire's heroes:

Une pauvreté noble est tout ce qui me reste.[2]

I suppose that *Giuditta,* as we used to call Mme. Pasta in Italian, used to lend him small sums of money from time to time to carry him over the worst of his money troubles.

I was not a great wit at that period, and yet there were some who envied me. M. de Perret, the spy in M. de Tracy's circle, knew of my friendly relations with Mme. Pasta; men in that business are always exchanging notes with their colleagues in the same line. In describing our friendship he managed to present it to the ladies in the rue d'Anjou under the most odious light. The conventional type of woman, who would never dream of having a love-affair herself, can never forgive a man for having an affair with an actress. I had once suffered from that stigma in Marseilles, but at that time Mme. Séraphie T . . . had some reason to discourage my visits every evening after she heard of my liaison with Mlle. Louason (a very spirited woman, who has since become Mme. de Barkoff).[3]

In the rue d'Anjou, which, after all, was the most respectable circle in which I moved, not even old M. de Tracy, the philosopher, forgave me for my supposed affair with an actress.

I am quick, hot-tempered, mad if you will, but excessively sincere both in friendship and in love up to the moment when I perceive the first sign of coldness. Then from the folly of a youth of sixteen I pass in the twinkling of an eye to the Machiavellianism of a man of fifty, and at the end of a week nothing is left of my former warmth but *melting ice,* a complete chill. (This has just happened to me again, *with Lady Angelica,* May 1832.)[4]

I was on the point of offering my undivided friendship to the members of the Tracy circle when I felt the first touch of frost in their attitude. From 1821 to 1830 I was therefore cold and Machiavellian in that house, that is, I proceeded with the utmost caution. Several friendships that showed some promise, as I see it now, were blighted in the unfavorable climate of the rue d'Anjou. To be sure the excellent Countess de Tracy—and I reproach myself bitterly for not having loved her more—did not assume that chilly manner toward me. However, when I returned from England for her sake, with an open heart and a great desire to be her sincere friend, I quelled my ardor deliberately, and resolved to be cold and calculating toward everyone else in the salon.

In Italy I used to adore the opera. The pleasantest hours of my life, by far, were spent at the opera house. And as a result of frequenting the *Scala* (the Milan opera house) I had become a kind of connoisseur of music.

When I was ten years old, my father, who had all sorts of religious and aristocratic prejudices, put every obstacle in the way of my studying music. Nevertheless at the age of sixteen I had a few singing lessons, and learned to play the violin and the clarinet. Only from this last instrument did I succeed in producing sounds that gave me pleasure. My teacher, a German named Hermann, who was a bit of a dandy, taught me to play a few simple little tunes. But who can tell? Perhaps he had known Mozart. This was in 1797, shortly after Mozart had died.

But at that time this great name had not been revealed to me. I was carried away by my great passion for mathematics, and for two years I had time for nothing else. Then I left for Paris, arriving there the day after the 18th Brumaire (November 10, 1799).

Since then, whenever the thought of studying music occurred to me, I realized that it was too late; in other words, the more I knew the less I wanted to study. I was appalled by the sounds I produced, inferior as they were to those of many

fourth-rate executants, who owe their slight technical skill—
which at best has a certain charm when you hear them play of
an evening in the country—only to the persistence with which
they split their own ears all morning long. Yet their morning
exercises, I suppose, do not really grate on their ears, because . . .
but metaphysical arguments of that sort might go on forever.

At any rate, I adored music, and was able to indulge this
passion to my heart's content in Germany, between 1806 and
1810, and later in Italy, from 1814 to 1821. In Italy I had
an opportunity to talk about music with old Mayer, young
Paccini, and various composers. On the other hand the instru-
mentalists, such as the Marquis Caraffa and the Viscontinis
of Milan, thought there was no sense in my observations.
It was as if, today, I should discuss political questions with a
sub-prefect.

It came as a great surprise to Count Daru, a real man of
letters from head to foot, who merited all the boredom of mem-
bership in the Academy of Inscriptions in 1828, to discover that
I could write a single page that might be of interest to anyone.
One day he bought a copy of one of my books from Delaunay,
who charged him forty francs because the edition was sold
out. His amazement was excruciatingly funny, the bookseller
related, when he told me the story.

"What! Forty francs!"

"Yes, count, and only as a favor to you. I'll be just as pleased
if you don't buy it at that price."

"Is it possible?" said the Academician, raising his eyes to
Heaven; "that child! As ignorant as a carp!"

He spoke in all sincerity. So the people who live at the
antipodes, gazing at the moon when it is only a slender cres-
cent in our skies, say to one another: "What a brilliant light!

The moon is almost at the full!" Count Daru, member of the French Academy, member of the Academy of Sciences, etc., etc., looked at nature and the heart of man from one pole, I from the opposite pole.

In much the same way Micheroux, who had a charming room next door to mine, on the third floor of the Hotel des Lillois, used to marvel that some people were willing to listen to me when I talked about music. When he learned that I had written a booklet on Haydn his astonishment knew no bounds. He gave the book his grudging approval—although it was too metaphysical, he said—but that I could have written it, that I should have been the author, I, incapable of striking a chord of the diminished seventh on the piano, it was this that made him open his eyes wide in disbelief. And he had very fine eyes, too, at least whenever by chance they showed a glint of expression.

This same surprise, that I have just described at some length, was manifested more or less by all the friends whom I frequented up to the period (1827) when I set about cultivating my wit.

Like a respectable woman turned harlot, I must constantly try to overcome the reserve that makes a gentleman reluctant to talk about himself. This book, however, is made up of nothing else. I did not foresee this sudden complication, which may cause me to abandon the whole project. I foresaw no other difficulty than that of having the courage to tell the truth about everything. But that is the least of my problems.

I lack precise details on the distant past, but I shall become less dry and verbose as I approach the period between 1826 and 1830. At that time my misfortunes drove me to become a wit, and I remember everything as if it were yesterday.

Owing to a strange quirk that has resulted in my being called a liar, or a queer duck, and above all an unpatriotic Frenchman, I find it very hard to enjoy the music sung in French theatres. Nevertheless, like all my friends in 1821, I was a devotee of the Opéra Comique.

It was there that Mme. Pasta used to play the leading role in *Tancrède, Othello, Romeo and Juliet* ... in a manner that has never been equaled, and was certainly not foreseen by the composers of those operas.

Talma, who may possibly be rated very highly by posterity, had the tragic spirit, to be sure, but he was foolish enough to fall into the most ridiculous affectations. But in spite of his total lack of intelligence, I suspect that he had also the servility needed for success, something that I found again after much seeking in the admirable and amiable Béranger.[5]

No doubt Talma was servile, mean, fawning, unctuous, etc., and perhaps exaggeratedly so to Mme. de Staël, who, since she was habitually and stupidly plagued by the thought of her own ugliness (if a word like "stupid" can be used in connection with that remarkable woman) constantly needed to be reassured on that score by the obvious and ever repeated protestations of her friends' esteem.

Like one of her lovers, the Prince de Talleyrand, Mme. de Staël knew *the art of succeeding in Paris*, and realized that she would have everything to gain by giving the seal of her approval to Talma, whose triumphs had been so great and so protracted that he was in danger of going out of *fashion*.

Talma's early triumphs were due to his boldness; he had the courage to make innovations, the only kind of courage that is rare among the French. He tried something new in Voltaire's *Brutus,* and also in that wretchedly overwritten play,

Charles IX, by M. de Chenier, produced shortly afterwards. An old actor I once knew, and a very bad one too, named Naudet, who was both a bore and a Royalist, was so offended by the young Talma's genius for innovation that he fought several duels with him. In truth I don't know where Talma got the idea or the courage to try so many new things, for when I saw him play he was far below that level.

In spite of his strident, unnatural voice, and the no less annoying and affected play of his double-jointed wrists, anyone in France who could be stirred by the fine tragic conceptions in the third act of Ducis' *Hamlet,* or by the great scenes in the last two acts of *Andromaque,*[6] had no alternative but to see Talma.

He had the tragic sense to an extraordinary degree. If in addition he had possessed a certain simplicity, and had been willing to take advice, he might have gone much farther; for example, he could have been just as sublime as Monvel in the part of Auguste (in *Cinna*). I am speaking here of things I have seen, and seen often, or at least with close attention, since I was an enthusiastic patron of the Théatre-Français for many years.

Fortunately for Talma, up to the time when a certain critic, a clever man who had much influence over the public (Abbé Geoffroy) wantonly destroyed his reputation as an actor, Mme. de Staël had been pleased to laud him to the skies. This eloquent woman took it upon herself to teach stupid people in what terms they should speak of Talma. As can well be imagined, she did this with her customary overemphasis. The name of Talma became known all over Europe.

His detestable affectations grew less and less apparent to the French, a race of sheep. I am not a sheep, and therefore I am a nobody.

No actor will ever be able to interpret the vague melancholy that stems from an inexorable fate as Talma did in the part of Oedipus. As Manlius he was quite the Roman; his delivery of "Take this, read it," and "Do you know Rutile's hand?" was superb, because in lines like those it was impossible for him to fall into the insufferable singsong of the alexandrines. How daring it was of me to entertain such opinions back in 1805! I am almost afraid to write such blasphemy even now (1832) when the two idols have fallen.[7]

However, in 1805 I predicted what would come to pass in 1832, and my triumph amazes and *stupefies* me (as in *Cinna*.) *Will I be equally successful with ti . . .*[8]

Talma's eternal singsong, his strident voice, his flapping wrists, his mincing gait all prevented me from enjoying his performance for five minutes in succession. I found myself constantly sifting the good from the bad in his acting, a most distracting process for the imagination. All illusion is destroyed when the intellect is brought into play.

The only perfect things in Talma were his head and his *dreamy gaze*. I might apply that expression "dreamy gaze" to Raphael's Madonnas and to Mlle. Virginie de Lafayette (Mme. Adolphe Périer), who had that type of beauty to a supreme degree. Her good grandmother, Countess de Tracy, was very proud of the girl.

I found the kind of tragic sense that appealed to me in Kean, and I worshipped him for it. He filled my eyes and my heart. I can still see him playing the part of Richard III and Othello.

But the only woman I have seen with the tragic sense, for me a far more moving experience, was Mme. Pasta, and in her it was absolutely pure and unalloyed. At home she would be silent and impassive. . . . But after one of her performances she would return from the theatre and collapse on the sofa, weeping and hysterical for several hours afterward.

Moreover, since her talent for tragic roles was combined with a fine voice, the emotion communicated through the visual sense was enhanced by what the ear recorded. Mme. Pasta had a trick of remaining in exactly the same pose for a comparatively long time, two or three seconds perhaps. Was this a convenience, or one more obstacle she gave herself to overcome? I have often wondered. I lean towards the belief that it was neither a help nor a hindrance. For Mme. Pasta the only problem was that of singing well.

The Chevalier Micheroux, Lussinge, di Fiori, Sutton-Sharp[9] and a few others shared my admiration for the *gran donna;* we never tired of discussing her last performance in *Romeo and Juliet,* as well as the stupid reviews of those paltry French critics who felt obliged to express an opinion on a thing as utterly foreign to the French character as *music.*

The Abbé Geoffroy, for example, though by far the wittiest and most learned of the newspaper critics, unblushingly called Mozart a *cheap tunesmith.* He wrote this in all sincerity, since he was not aware of merit in any composers save *Grétry* and *Monsigny,* whose music he had *learned* to like.

Kind reader, make sure you understand the meaning of that word "learned," for it represents the history of music in France.

Judge then of the asinine reviews written in 1822 by all the raffish journalists who were so much inferior to M. Geoffroy. The articles of this clever schoolmaster have recently been collected in book form, but they say that as a miscellany it falls flat. When dished up impromptu, twice a week, his pieces were superb, infinitely superior to the ponderous reviews of someone like M. Hoffman or M. Feletz, although these might stand up better if published as a collection of essays than the playful sketches by Geoffrey. When these critics were all at the height of their fame I used to go to the Café Hardy, which was then very fashionable, and lunch on delicious kidneys *en brochette*. Well, on the days when I found no article by Geoffroy in the paper, my luncheon lost its flavor.

Geoffroy used to dash off these little essays while listening to the reading of Latin themes by his pupils at the . . . School, where he was a teacher. One day, when he brought some of his students to a café near the Bastille for a glass of beer, the boys were delighted to come upon a newspaper that revealed what kept their teacher so busy writing in class, holding the paper up to the tip of his nose because he was so very nearsighted.

It was also thanks to Geoffroy's myopia that Talma was credited with his famous "dreamy gaze," which was supposed to indicate such depth of soul (a state of inward concentration, sustained until something interesting forcibly drew his attention outward).

There is one thing that diminishes Mme. Pasta's talent, I find. It was a simple matter for her to be natural when portraying a lofty soul because it was innate in her.

For example, she was known to be avaricious, or, one might say, economical for good reason, since she had a prodigal husband. Well, in one month alone, she would give away two hundred francs to destitute Italian refugees. And among these were several graceless characters, the sort of men who would normally cure you of the habit of alms-giving, such as Gianonne, the poet from Modena, whom Heaven forgive for his sins. What a strange look he gave one!

M. di Fiori, he who resembled Jupiter Mansuetus, and who had been condemned to death in Naples when he was only twenty-three, was charged with distributing Mme. Pasta's charities in the most judicious manner. He alone knew how large they were at the time, and he only told me about them long afterward, in confidence. I see in today's paper (June 1832) that the Queen of France has announced publicly that she recently sent a donation of seventy francs to an old woman.

Chapter VIII

⁓

Aside from the impudence required to talk about myself constantly, I find writing these memoirs trying for another reason: how many of the bold observations here set down in fear and trembling will be merely dull platitudes ten years after my death, supposing that Heaven grants me a rather respectable life-span of eighty or ninety years!

On the other hand, it is a joy to write of General Foy and Mme. Pasta, of Lord Byron and Napoleon and all the great or at any rate distinguished persons it has been my good fortune to know and who have condescended to speak to me!

For the rest, if the reader is envious of my good fortune in this respect, like my contemporaries, he may console himself with the reflection that few of the great men I admired so much divined my true character. I suspect that they may even have found me less entertaining than other men; perhaps they only saw in me an *exaggerated sentimentalist.*

Indeed one could scarcely be rated much lower than that. It was only after I began to display some wit that I began to be appreciated, and much beyond my deserts. General Foy, Mme. Pasta, M. de Tracy, Canova, none of these *divined* (I seem to be obsessed by that foolish word "divined") that my heart brimmed over with kindness—I have the bump of kindness according to Gall's system of phrenology—or that I had an exalted spirit, one that was equal to comprehending them.

One of the men who did not understand me, and on the whole the man I liked perhaps most of all (he realized my "ideal," as some windy fool or other has phrased it) was Andrea Corner of Venice, former aide-de-camp to Prince Eugene at Milan.

In 1811 I was an intimate friend of Count *Widmann,* captain of a company of Venetian guardsmen (I was the lover of his mistress). When I ran into him again in Moscow, he asked me point-blank to make him a senator of the kingdom of Italy, in the belief that I was the favorite of my cousin, Count Daru, who as a matter of fact never cared for me at all, but quite the contrary. At any rate, in 1811 Widmann introduced me to Corner, who impressed me greatly by his resemblance to one of those fine heads painted by Veronese.

People say that Count Corner squandered a fortune of five million francs in his time. He was capable of the most generous acts, quite unlike a man of the world in France. As for his courage, he was decorated twice by Napoleon in person (with the iron cross and the Legion of Honor).

It was he who made that extraordinarily naïve exclamation at four o'clock in the afternoon of the battle of the Moscow River (September 7, 1812): "Will this confounded battle never end?" Widmann or Migliorini reported this to me the following day.

None of the brave but rather affected Frenchmen I knew in the army at the time, such as General de Caulaincourt, General Monbrun, or others, would have dared come out with such a remark, not even the Duke of Frioul (Michel Duroc). Although Frioul was a man of rare simplicity of character, yet in this, as in the liveliness of his mind, he was much beneath Andrea Corner.

This delightful man, now growing bald, was living in poverty in Paris at the period I am describing. He was destitute at the age of thirty-eight, an age when time begins to weigh on your hands if you are disillusioned. Then too—and so far as I know this was his only fault—at times he used to be seen in the garden of the Palais Royale at nightfall, a little under the influence of liquor. This often happens to illustrious men at a low ebb in their fortunes: unthroned princes, for example, or Mr. Pitt on beholding the triumphs of Napoleon, hearing the outcome of the battle of Austerlitz.

JULY 2, 1832.

Lussinge, the most prudent man I have ever known, was extremely reluctant as a rule to introduce me to his friends, as he wished to make sure that he would always have me for a companion in his morning walks.

Nevertheless he did take me to the house of M. de Maisonnette, one of the oddest characters I have ever met in Paris.[1]

He is thin and dark, quite short, like a Spaniard, with bold eyes and a sort of impetuous courage.

Maisonnette has much in common with men like Vitet, Leon Pillet, Saint-Marc Girardin and other hack writers attached to the Treasury Department, in his ability to dash off in the course of an evening an article thirty pages long, written in an elegant and prolix style, defending some political thesis for a Cabinet minister who had sent him a note with the merest hint of what he wanted as late as six o'clock that afternoon. The curious, the incredible thing is that Maisonnette always believes in what he writes. He has devoted himself in turn to M. Decazes, M. de Villèle, and finally to M. de Martignac—to the point of being willing to sacrifice his life for them. M. de Martignac, at any rate, was a likable person.[2]

Many a time I have tried to fathom Maisonnette. At times I have thought I discerned a complete want of logic in the man, and at others a breakdown of all moral sense, a stifling of any slight twinge of conscience that might trouble him at moments. All of his behavior seems to be based on the one great axiom: I must survive.

Maisonnette has no conception of the duties of a citizen. He looks on all that as I look on the relations between men and angels, which M. Ancillon, at present minister to Berlin, believes in so devoutly. Maisonnette shows as much concern for the duties of the citizen as Dominique[3] has for the obligations of religion.

If at times the constant reiteration of the words "honor" and "loyalty" awakens some slight feeling of remorse in his breast, he squares himself with his conscience by his chivalrous devotion to his friends. Even though I had neglected him for six months at a stretch, I would feel free to rouse him up at five o'clock in the morning to go out and beg some favor for me. He would also go to the North Pole to seek out and fight a duel with any man who had cast some reflection on his honor as a man of breeding.

He never wearied his brain with Utopian plans for the public welfare, or wise constitutions, but he was a veritable storehouse of all sorts of little state secrets. One evening when Lussinge, Gazul and I were speaking of M. de Jouy, then the most fashionable author of the day, the so-called successor of Voltaire, Maisonnette rose and went searching through his voluminous collection of papers for the very letter in which M. de Jouy asked the Bourbons for the Cross of Saint-Louis.

It took him less than two minutes to find this document, so out of keeping with the unmitigated virtue M. de Jouy, as a devout liberal, arrogated to himself.

Since Maisonnette was neither a knave, a coward, or a Jesuit like the editors of the *Journal des Débats,* those gentlemen were shocked when they learned that M. de Villèle, who was known as a practical fellow, paid him fifteen or twenty thousand francs for his services.

The men in the rue des Prêtres[4] considered Maisonnette a fool, but his large salary, like the laurels of Miltiades, kept them awake at night.

After we had laughed over the letter of Jouy, which he had written when he was adjutant general, Maisonnette remarked: "Isn't it strange that the two leading figures in literature and liberal politics today should both be named Etienne?"[5]

As a matter of fact, M. de Jouy took his name from the town of Jouy, where he was born, the son of a merchant whose patronymic was Etienne. Endowed by nature with an audacity that the poor Germans find impossible to understand, young Etienne when he was only fourteen years old left Jouy, which is near Versailles, to go to India. There he assumed the name of Etienne de Jouy, then E. de Jouy, and at last, simply de Jouy. He actually rose to be a captain, and later some member of the Convention, I believe, commissioned him a colonel. Although he was a brave fellow, he served only a short time or not at all. In appearance he was quite prepossessing.

One day in India he and several of his friends entered a temple to escape from the frightful heat. There they found a priestess, a kind of vestal virgin. M. de Jouy thought it a great joke to render her faithless to Brahma on the very altar of her god.

When the Hindus discovered what had happened, they were up in arms at once, and flocking to the temple, cut off the hands and then the head of the vestal virgin. They also hacked to pieces one of the French officers, but the dead man's comrade, M. de Jouy, the author of *Scylla,* managed to mount his horse and ride off, and in fact still gallops about today.

Before M. de Jouy came to apply his talents for intrigue to literature, he was, toward 1810, secretary-general of the Prefecture of Brussels. There, as I have heard, he was the lover of the prefect's wife, and the chief factotum of the prefect himself, M. de Pontécoulant, a man of remarkable intelligence. Between the two of them they suppressed all mendicancy, which is rife everywhere and particularly in Belgium, a predominantly Catholic country.

When the Great Man fell, M. de Jouy asked the Bourbons for the Cross of Saint-Louis, and on its being refused by the reigning imbeciles, proceeded to make a laughing stock of them in his writings. Thereby he did them more harm than all the highly paid scriveners of the *Journal des Débats* did them good. Hence the rage of the *Journal des Débats* against *Minerve.*[6]

For five or six years M. de Jouy *believed* sincerely that he was Voltaire's successor, because he had written *l'Ermite de la Chaussée d'Antin,* a book well-suited to the middle-class French mind and to the naïve curiosity of the Germans, and so he kept a bust of Voltaire in the garden of his house in the rue des Trois Frères.

Since 1829 the literary men of the Romantic School in France, who have even less brains than M. de Jouy, dismiss him as the *Cotin*[7] of the period (after Boileau) and his old age has been soured *(amaregiata)* by the memory of the extraordinary fame he enjoyed in his ripe years.

When I arrived in Paris in 1821, he shared the dictatorship of the literary world with another dolt infinitely more crude than he, M. A.-V. Arnault, member of the Institute, and Mme. Brac's lover. I used to meet M. Arnault frequently at the home of Mme. Cuvier, who was the sister of his mistress. He had about as much wit as a drunken navvy. And yet he wrote the following pretty verses:

> *Où vas-tu, feuille de chêne?*
> *—Je vais où le vent me mène.*[8]

He wrote this on the eve of his departure into exile, his personal misfortunes having suddenly put some life into that feather-brain of his. When I knew him around 1811, at the home of Count Daru, whom he later received at the French Academy, he was thoroughly base and groveling. M. de Jouy, a much nicer fellow, sold what remained of his masculine charms to Mme. Davilliers, the oldest and dreariest of all the coquettes of that era. She was or still is far more ridiculous than Countess Baraguey d'Hilliers, who, at the tender age of fifty-seven, went about recruiting her lovers from among young men of wit. I do not know whether it was because of any claims I might have to such a title that I was once obliged to flee from her clutches at the home of Mme. Dubignon. She once took that clown, de Masson (former Master of Petitions)[9] as her lover, and when one of my women friends said to her: "What! such an ugly creature!" she replied:

"I took him for his mind."

The cream of the joke is that de Masson, M. Beugnot's gloomy secretary, had no more mind than he had beauty. And yet one cannot deny that he has a certain adroitness, an ability to advance himself by biding his time and swallowing all sorts of toads, and a knowledge, not so much of finance, as of the routine financial operations of the state. Simpletons confuse the two things.

One day when I was admiring Mme. d'Hilliers' arms—she has lovely arms for a woman of her age—she said to me:

"I will teach you how to use your talents to make your fortune. Without help you will break your neck."

I lacked the sense to understand her then. But I often stared at the old countess because she wore such charming frocks, designed by Victorine. I am captivated by beautiful clothes; they give me the greatest sensual pleasure. Mme. N. C. D. developed my taste for such things long ago, a taste linked in my mind with delightful memories of Cideville.[10]

It was Mme. Baraguey d'Hilliers, as I recall, who told me that the author[11] of a delicious little song, one I liked so much that I carried it about in my pocket, used to compose little verses for the birthdays of those two old monkeys, Jouy and Arnault, and also the frightful Mme. Davilliers.

I have never had a gift for that sort of thing, but neither could I have written *Le Roi d'Yvetot, Le Sénateur, La Grand'mère.*

M. de Béranger, content with having acquired the name of a great poet (a title he well deserved) by flattering these baboons, would not stoop to flatter the government of Louis-Philippe, to which so many other liberals have sold out.

CHAPTER IX

BUT I MUST RETURN TO A LITTLE GARDEN IN THE RUE
Caumartin. There, every summer evening, several bottles of
well-cooled beer were kept in readiness for us by a tall, handsome woman, Mme. Romance. Mme. Romance was separated
from her husband, a scurvy printer, and had become the mistress of Maisonnette, who had bought her from the aforemen-
tioned husband for two or three thousand francs.[1]

Lussinge and I went there frequently. While walking on
the boulevard in the evening after dinner, we often ran into
M. Darbelles, a childhood friend of ours, now six feet tall and
a great bore, who used to hold forth on the subject of Gebelin[2]
and declare his belief in progress through science.

When we met him he was usually on his way to call on his
mother in the rue Caumartin, and in order to get rid of him we
would turn into Maisonnette's house.

That summer I began to rouse myself up a bit to what was
going on about me. For five or six hours at a stretch I managed
to put the thought of Milan out of my mind, but the moment of
waking, alone, was still bitter for me. Sometimes I would stay
abed till midday, brooding darkly.

I would therefore listen attentively as Maisonnette described how *power,* the only real force in the world, was distributed in Paris at that time, in 1821. Whenever I arrive in a city, I always try to find out: 1) who are the twelve prettiest women; 2) who are the twelve richest men; 3) what man there has the power to have me hanged.

Maisonnette answered these questions fairly well. What was surprising to me was that he was sincerely enamored of the word *King.* To a Frenchman, he would say rapturously, raising his little black eyes fervently to Heaven, how much meaning there is in that word *King!*

When Maisonnette was a teacher of rhetoric back in 1811, he impulsively dismissed his class the day the King of Rome was born. In 1815 he wrote a pamphlet in favor of the Bourbons. M. Decazes read it, sent for him, and made him his political ghost-writer at a salary of six thousand francs a year. Today Maisonnette is an extremely useful man for any prime minister to have at his beck and call, for he has an encyclopedic knowledge, detailed and precise, of all the secret political intrigues in Paris from 1815 to 1832.

I did not at first appreciate Maisonnette's talents, which can be properly estimated only after you have drawn him out. I would say to myself: He's making game of someone here. Am I the butt? Can it be Lussinge? Or it is that poor young fellow in the gray frock-coat, that ugly youth with the turned-up nose? There was something quite impertinent, something extremely unpleasant about that young man. His eyes, small and cold, had a fixed expression and that expression was malicious.

Such was my first reaction to one who is today my best friend. I am not too sure of his heart, but I am certain of the talent of Count Gazul,[3] whose name is now so well-known. It made me happy for two days to receive a letter from him last week. When I first met him he must have been only eighteen years old, having been born, as I remember, in 1804.*

Now I tend to agree with Buffon that we take after our mothers in large part, all joking aside about uncertain paternity, a rare thing, in any case, for the first child. This theory seems confirmed by the case of Count Gazul. His mother is a woman of lively, typically French humor, with a superior mind. Like her son, she impresses me as one who would be susceptible to tender feelings no more than once a year. In most of M. Gazul's works likewise I find a certain *coldness*, but I am counting on a change in the future.

At the time I met him in the pretty little garden in the rue Caumartin, Gazul was studying rhetoric with the most abominable of teachers. It is surprising to find the word *abominable* linked with the name of Maisonnette, who is the best of men. But his taste in the arts was really abominable—he admired the false, the brilliant, the cheap sort of thing above all.

He had been a pupil of M. Luce de Lancival, whom I met in my earliest youth at the home of M. de Maisonneuve. Maisonneuve always refused to publish his tragedies, although they had had a great success on the stage. A good fellow, he once had the great kindness to tell me that I would have a superior mind.

"You mean a *superior pride*," laughed Martial Daru, who considered me almost stupid. But I forgave him for all that, for it was he who once brought me to see Clotilde, then the prima ballerina at the Opéra. Sometimes—and what great days they were for me!—when I visited her in her dressing room at the

---

* Made 14 pages on July 2 from five to seven o'clock. I could not have worked this way on an imaginative project like *Le Rouge et le Noir*.
—Beyle.

Opéra, she would change her costume right before my eyes, the eyes of a fourth-form schoolboy. What an experience for a lad from the provinces!

Luce de Lancival had a wooden leg and a pleasant disposition, but for the rest, he was a man who was capable of inserting a pun in a tragedy. I imagine that Dorat had the same attitude towards the arts.[4] But a more exact parallel perhaps would be one of Boucher's shepherd scenes. Will there still be paintings by Boucher in the Museum by 1860?

Maisonnette had been the pupil of Luce de Lancival, and Gazul was the pupil of Maisonnette, just as Carracio was the pupil of Calvart, the Flemish painter.

Aside from his courage, aside from his great and sincere passion for the reigning prime minister, Maisonnette had another quality I admired: he drew twenty-two thousand francs a year from the government for proving to the French people that the Bourbons were worthy of adoration, and he somehow managed to spend thirty thousand.

After having worked, sometimes, twelve hours at a stretch, to bring the French public around to the right view of things, Maisonnette would then go to see some respectable woman of the lower classes and offer her five hundred francs to go to bed with him. He was small and ugly, but he had so much Spanish fire in him that after three visits these women would forget his odd face and see only the sublime beauty of the five-hundred-franc note.

I must add something here for the benefit of any respectable woman whose eye may fall on these pages, if such there should ever be: first, five hundred francs in 1822 would be the equivalent of a thousand in 1872; and second, a charming little street vendor once confessed to me that before receiving the five-hundred-franc note from Maisonnette, she had never had as much as fifty francs to herself.

Rich people are both very unjust and very ridiculous when they thunder against all the sins and crimes committed for the sake of money. Consider what sordid things they themselves do, the ten years they spend currying favor at court, just to win a portfolio in the cabinet. Consider the life of the Duke Decazes between 1820, when he fell from power after the Louvel affair, and the present.

There I was then in 1822, spending three evenings a week at the Opéra Comique and one or two at Maisonnette's house in the rue Caumartin. Whenever I have felt dejected, the evening hours have always been the unhappiest time of day for me. If there was a performance at the Opéra, however, I was sure to be at Mme. Pasta's afterwards, with Lussinge, Micheraux, Fiori and the others, from midnight until two o'clock in the morning.

I narrowly missed fighting a duel with one lively and gallant fellow who wanted me to introduce him to Mme. Pasta. The man in question was Edouard Edwards, my traveling companion in England, the only Englishman in the world with a fun-loving spirit, who had offered to fight a duel on my behalf in London.

You will not have forgotten that Edwards once pointed out a shameful oversight on my part: that of not having paid enough attention to an offensive remark made by a boorish ship captain at Calais.

Nevertheless I refused to present him to Mme. Pasta. It was nine o'clock when he made his request, and at nine o'clock in the evening poor Edouard was not the man he was in the morning.

"You know, my dear B . . ." he said, "I might take that as an insult."

"You know, my dear Edwards," I replied, "that I have as much pride as you, and that your opinions are a matter of complete indifference to me, etc."

This was going pretty far, but I am a fairly good marksman, and can hit nine sitting ducks out of twelve. (M. Prosper Mérimée saw me do this at the Luxembourg shooting-gallery.) Edwards is a good marksman too, but perhaps not quite as good as I am.

In the end this quarrel strengthened our friendship. I remember the incident very well because a day or so later, with characteristic thoughtlessness, I asked him to introduce me to his famous brother, Doctor Edwards, who was much talked about in 1822. Doctor Edwards used to kill a thousand frogs a month in the course of his experiments, and according to rumor was on the brink of discovering how we breathe and how to cure the chest ailments of pretty women. Do you know that every year eleven hundred young women die of a chill they catch on leaving the ballroom? I have seen the official figures.

Now Doctor Edwards, a scientist, of quiet and studious habits, held a very low opinion of the friends of his brother Edouard. In the first place the doctor had sixteen brothers and my friend was the black sheep of the family. It was because of his too boisterous humor and his inability to refrain from indulging in the lowest kind of practical joke that I had been reluctant to bring him to Mme. Pasta's.

Young Edwards had a large head, fine roving eyes, and the bonniest golden locks I have ever seen. If not for his confounded mania of trying always to shine as a wit, just like a Frenchman, he would have been an extremely likable fellow, and might have enjoyed the most gratifying success with women, as I shall explain later in speaking of *Eugény*.[5]

But *Eugény* is still so young that perhaps it's wrong to mention her in these memoirs, which may be published ten years after my death. However, if I extend the period to twenty years, all the *fine shadings of my life* will have lost their value, and the reader will see only the large masses. But where the deuce are the large *masses* in this pen sketch? I must look into this.

Taking a noble revenge on me, for he had a generous spirit when it was not drowned in fifty glasses of brandy, Edwards put himself out to obtain permission to present me to his brother.

On my first visit I found myself in a little parlor that was the quintessence of the bourgeois, presided over by a most virtuous woman whose talk was on a high moral plane, and whom I mistook for a Quakeress. The doctor himself was a man of rare qualities hidden in a puny little body whose life seemed to be ebbing away. The room was so dim you couldn't see a thing (12 rue du Helder). They received me coolly enough.

What the deuce had made me ask for an introduction! It had been a sudden caprice, a foolish whim. At bottom, if there was anything I longed for, it was to know my fellow-men. Every month or so I would remember this, but I would have to wait until the tastes, the passions, the sudden escapades that took up my time were submerged, leaving the surface of the waters calm so that this picture of mankind might appear clearly. Then I would say to myself, I am not like X . . . and Y . . . , those coxcombs of my acquaintance. I do not choose my friends.

I take at random, whatever fate throws in my path.

For ten years that thought has been my pride.

It took me three years and all my tact to overcome the repugnance and dread I inspired in Mme. Edwards' salon. I was taken for a Don Juan (see Mozart and Molière), for an incorrigible seducer with a satanic mind. I am sure it would have required less effort on my part to be tolerated in the salon of Mme. de Talaru, or Mme. de Duras, or Mme. de Broglie, who received the bourgeoisie in her house quite as a matter of course, or Mme. Guizot, whom I admired so much (I am referring to the former Mlle. Pauline de Meulan) or even in the salon of Mme. Récamier.[6]

But in 1822 I did not understand the full importance of the answer to the question people always ask about the author of a book they read: *What manner of man is he?*

I was spared the disdain of some by the answer usually given in my case: "He visits Mme. de Tracy frequently." In 1829 good society felt obliged to look down on a man who, rightly or wrongly, was credited with some wit in his writings. Worldly people were frightened by that sort of thing, and became incapable of judging a work on its merits. What sort of reception would I have had if the answer to the above question had been: "He visits Mme. de Duras (formerly Mlle. de Kersaint) frequently?"

Ah well, even today, when I know the importance of such connections, or rather because I appreciate their importance fully, I would be willing to quit fashionable salons. (I have just quit going to the salon of Lady Holye[7] ... in 1832.)

But I was faithful to the salon of Doctor Edwards, who was not a genial man, as one is faithful to an ugly mistress, because I felt free to absent myself from it on Wednesdays (Mme. Edwards' at-home day).

I can bear anything on the spur of the moment, but if I am told that tomorrow I must resign myself to being bored at such and such an hour, my imagination magnifies the threat until I would rather jump out of the window than be forced to attend a dreary gathering.

At the home of the Edwards I made the acquaintance of Mr. Stritch, a gloomy, impassive but extremely upright man who was a victim of the British aristocracy, for he was an Irishman and a lawyer. And yet, in line with his code of honor, he defended all the prejudices that had been instilled and cultivated in the minds of Englishmen by the aristocracy.

I found this same contradiction, combined with the highest rectitude and delicacy, in Mr. Rogers, who lives near Birmingham (where I spent some time with him in August 1826).[8]

In this matter of accepting the ideas of the aristocracy the average Englishman is almost as illogical as the average German, which is no light accusation.

An Englishman, whose reasoning power is so admirable in matters of finance and in everything pertaining to the art of making money, loses his bearings the moment he is asked to deal with higher subjects, abstract principles, let us say, or anything *not directly concerned with making money*. In their discussion of great literature they sound like imbeciles, for the same reason that we have imbeciles in the diplomatic service OF THE KING OF FRENCH,[9] namely, because their critics, like our diplomats, are chosen from among a small number of men, from a select group.

A dealer in cotton thread from Manchester may have the mental qualifications to judge the genius of Shakespeare and Cervantes (two great men who died on the same day, April 16, 1616, I believe), but such a man would reproach himself for wasting time if he opened a book not bearing directly on the cotton business, its export to Germany, when the thread is to be spun, etc., etc.

In the same way the *King of French* chooses his diplomats from among young men of high station or fortune. But we must look for ability where men like M. Thiers are produced (although he sold out in 1830). He is the son of a small tradesman at Aix-en-Provence.

When the summer of 1822 came around, a year or so after my departure from Milan, I thought only rarely of withdrawing voluntarily from this world. My days began to be filled little by little, not so much with pleasant things as with activities of one kind or another, and these interposed themselves between me and the happiness that had been the object of my worship.

I had two extremely innocent diversions at this time: 1) My morning stroll after breakfast with Lussinge or some other acquaintance; there were eight or ten such, all chance companions, as usual; and 2) dropping in at Galignani's bookshop to read the English newspapers in his garden after the weather turned hot. It was there that I reread with delight four or five novels of Walter Scott. The first, in which the characters Henry Morton and Sergeant Boswell appear (*Old Mortality*, I think) used to bring back vivid memories of Volterra.[10] I had often dipped into it while waiting for Metilda in Florence, at Molini's bookshop on the Arno. I reread it now in recollection of 1818.

In the course of long arguments I had with Lussinge on this subject, I would maintain that fully a third of the credit for the works of Sir Walter Scott should go by rights to some secretary who made landscape sketches for him after nature. I found him then, as I find him today, weak in the description of passion, in knowledge of the human heart. Will posterity confirm the judgment of my contemporaries who place the staunch Tory Baronet immediately after Shakespeare?

I abhor Scott personally, and have refused to meet him on several occasions (in Paris, through M. de Mirbel, in Naples in 1832, and in Rome the same year).

Fox gave him a post bringing fifty or a hundred thousand francs a year, and from then on he began slyly to slander Lord Byron, who profited by this great lesson in hypocrisy, as witnessed by the letter Lord Byron wrote me in 1823.[11]

Kind reader, have you ever seen a silkworm that has devoured all the mulberry leaves it can hold? The ugly insect can eat no more; it is ready to crawl up and weave its silken cage. The comparison is not very dignified, but it is so very apt! Such is the beast called "writer." For anyone who has had a taste of the absorbing occupation of writing, there is only a secondary pleasure to be extracted from reading. Often, while at work, I have thought it was only two o'clock when a glance at the clock showed that it was half-past six. This is my only excuse for having blackened so much paper with ink.

As my spirits revived in the summer of 1822, I made plans to publish a book entitled *l'Amour* that I had scrawled in pencil in Milan as I wandered about and thought of Metilda.

I had counted on rewriting it in Paris, for it was badly in need of revision. But it made me too unhappy to concentrate on that sort of thing. It was like rubbing my hand roughly over the scar of a recent wound. So I merely transcribed in ink those sections of the manuscript that were written in pencil.

My friend Edwards found me a bookseller (M. Mongie) who gave me nothing for the manuscript but promised me half of the profits, if there should ever be any to divide.[12]

Today, now that by some chance I wear gold braid,[13] I receive letters from booksellers I have never heard of (one from a M. Thiévoz, I believe, in June 1832) who offer to pay cash for my manuscripts.

I had no notion of the low character of the whole publishing fraternity. What I have learned since has shocked me and almost made me give up writing. The intrigues of M. Hugo (see the *Gazette des Tribunaux* of 1831 for his suit against the bookseller Bossan or Placan) the maneuvers of M. de Chateaubriand, the bargaining of M. Béranger are all quite justifiable, I am convinced. That great poet, Béranger, for example, had been dismissed by the Bourbons from his post at the Ministry of the Interior, even though it brought him only 1800 francs a year.

The stupidity of the Bourbons now stands forth in all the light of day. If they had not stooped to dismiss a poor clerk for writing a song that was intended to be funny rather than malicious, he would not have developed his great talent, and would not have become the glorious poet we know today, one of the most powerful forces at work to drive the Bourbons out. Béranger expressed in humorous terms the scorn felt by the French people for that *putrid* throne. It was thus that the Bourbons were described by the Queen of Spain, she who died in Rome, the friend of the Prince of Peace.

I had occasion to know something of that Court, but it bores me to write of anything but the analysis of the human heart. If I had happened to have a secretary, I might have been another kind of author.

But we have plenty of that sort, says the devil's advocate.

The old Queen of Spain brought her confessor along with her to Rome. This confessor had as his mistress the stepdaughter of the cook of the French Academy. Well along in years, but still a ladies' man, this Spanish priest was indiscreet enough to tell someone (I cannot furnish all the amusing details here, since the mummers in this masque are still alive) that Ferdinand VII was not the son of Charles IV, and that this had been one of the great sins of the old Queen. She was dead when he made this revelation, but a spy got wind of what he had said. Ferdinand had the old man brought home from Rome, but instead of finishing him off with poison, threw him into the dungeons of the Presidium after I know not what counter-intrigue.

Dare I tell of the malady of that old Queen, who was a woman of so much good sense? I heard the story in Rome either in 1817 or 1824. As a result of certain gallantries from whose effects she was never wholly cured, she broke one of her bones every time she fell down. The poor woman, being a queen, was ashamed of these frequent accidents but dared not seek a complete cure. At the Court of Napoleon in 1811 I ran into several unfortunates who had the same symptoms. I myself was very well acquainted, alas, with the excellent Dr. Cuillerier (I mean the uncle or the father, in short, the old man, not the young man of that name, who strikes me as a fool). I brought three women to him for treatment (at 26 rue de l'Odéon) two of whom I blindfolded.

When I saw him a few days later he told me that they had shown signs of fever (the effect of shame, not of the malady). A man of perfect good breeding, he had never raised his eyes to look them in the face.

It is always fortunate for the Bourbon tribe to be rid of a monster like Ferdinand VII. Nevertheless, the Duke de Laval, a very cultivated man, though an aristocrat and a duke (which is the equivalent of having two mental diseases) deemed it an honor to be able to tell me of his friendship with Ferdinand VII. And yet he had been ambassador at the court of Spain for three years!

I am reminded here of the great hatred Louis XVI felt for Franklin. Devising a typically Bourbon manner of taking vengeance on him, the king had the face of the venerable old man painted on the inside of a porcelain chamber pot.

It was Mme. Campon who told us that anecdote one evening at the home of Mme. Cardon (rue de Lille, corner of the rue de Bellechasse) after the 18th Brumaire. The memoirs of the court that we used to read at Mme. Cardon's house in those days were quite the opposite of the tearful rhapsodies that moved the hearts of elegant young women of the Faubourg Saint-Honoré later (which was what brought about my disillusionment on the score of one of them towards 1827).[14]

Chapter X

So there i was with an occupation at last in the summer of 1822: correcting the proofs of *l'Amour*. It was to be a duodecimo volume, printed on bad paper, but M. Mongie, all indignation, swore to me that he had been cheated on the quality. In 1822 I did not understand the tricks of booksellers. The only one with whom I had had dealings theretofore was M. Firmin Didot, whom I paid for the paper used in my books according to his price-list. M. Mongie chuckled over my ignorance when he heard this.

"Ah, you don't *know the game!*" he would gasp, convulsed with laughter, and then he would compare me to old hands like Ancelot, Vitet, and other professional writers.

Well, I discovered later that M. Mongie was far from being the most honest of booksellers. And what shall I say of my friend M. Sautelet, the young lawyer, who was my friend, that is to say, before he became a bookseller?

The poor devil died of chagrin when his mistress, a rich widow by the name of Mme. Bonnet or Bourdet, or some such "aristocratic" cognomen, left him for a young peer of France (the title "peer of France" was beginning to have quite a pleasant sound in 1828). This fortunate peer, I believe was M. Pérignon, who had been the lover of my friend Mlle. Vigano, daughter of the great Vigano (in 1820, as I remember).

It was a very risky thing for me to correct the proofs of a book that recalled so many of the feelings I had experienced in Italy. In a moment of weakness I rented a room at Montmorency, and I used to go there in the afternoon, a two-hour trip by the diligence that left from the rue Saint-Denis. As we passed through the woods, especially those to the left of la Sablonnière, and climbed the hill, I would correct my proofs. I nearly went mad.

A wild desire to return to Milan, which I had so often suppressed, now came back to me with overpowering force. How I was able to resist it I do not know.

The dominance of an all-absorbing passion, concentrated on one object, has blotted out the memory of everything I saw at Montmorency. After all these years I recall nothing distinctly but the shape of the trees in a certain part of the woods.

What people call the valley of Montmorency is only a promontory jutting out toward the Seine valley in the direction of the dome of the Invalides.

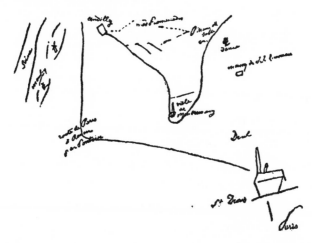

When Lanfranco depicted a cupola that was a hundred and fifty feet high in one of his paintings, he exaggerated certain features of the structure. *"L'aria depinge,"* he used to say (the air itself paints).

In the same way, since men will be far more disillusioned about Kings, nobles and priests in 1870 than they are today, I am tempted to exaggerate certain unpleasant features of those vermin of the human species. But I abstain, because to write thus would be *false to the truth*.

> False to his bed!
> *Cymbeline*

If only I had a secretary to whom I could dictate, I would put down many facts and anecdotes—not judgments—about various Kings, nobles and priests! But having written twenty-seven pages today, I am too tired to relate all the anecdotes that besiege my mind.

JULY 4.

I also went out to Corbeil frequently, to correct the proofs of *l'Amour* in the park of Mme. Doligny's chateau.

There I was able to avoid any sad reveries, and as soon as my work was done for the day I could go in to her drawing room.

In 1824 I was within reach of happiness. Whenever I thought of France during the six or seven years I spent in Milan, hoping never to see Paris again—sullied as it was by the Bourbons—nor France either for that matter, I used to say to myself: Only one woman could reconcile me to my country, Countess Fanny Bertois.[1]

I loved her dearly in 1824. But we had felt warmly towards each other ever since 1814, when I had seen her come running into her mother's house (the Marquise de N . . .) to get news of the battle of Montmirail or Champaubert at six o'clock in the morning, the day after the battle.

At any rate, Mme. Bertois was visiting her friend Mme. Doligny in the country at this period. When at length I decided to show my sorry face at her door, Mme. Doligny met me with:

"Mme. Bertois was hoping you would come. She left me only the day before yesterday because a tragedy has befallen her family. She has just lost one of her charming daughters."

In the mouth of a woman as keen as Mme. Doligny, these words had great significance. As far back as 1814 she had said to me: "Mme. Bertois appreciates all your good qualities."

In 1822 or 1823, Mme. Bertois had the kindness to love me a little. One day Mme. Doligny said to her: "Your glance is often fixed on Beyle, I see; if he had a better figure he would have told you long ago that he loved you."

This was not quite correct. In my melancholy mood I enjoyed gazing into the fine eyes of Mme. Bertois. But I was too stupid to understand that I could have gone any further. I did not ask myself: why does that young woman look at me that way? I had forgotten completely the excellent lessons in love that my uncle Gagnon and my friend and patron Martial Daru had given me once upon a time.

My uncle Gagnon, who was born in Grenoble around 1765, was a charming man. His conversation, which to most men sounded like some overwritten novel of the fashionable world, was perfectly delightful to the ears of women. He was always amusing, full of delicacy, bubbling over with the kind of talk that implies everything and nothing. He lacked the high spirits, so frightening to many people, that I unfortunately possess. It would be hard to find a man more personable and less rational than my uncle Gagnon. Hence he never made his mark among men. The younger men envied him without being able to imitate him. Men of *ripe age,* as they say in Grenoble, found him a *light* fellow. That word alone is enough to damn a man. Although he was a staunch Royalist, like all the rest of my family in 1815, and even though he had emigrated in 1792, my uncle was never allowed to plead before the royal law-court in Grenoble, despite the fact that the court was filled with rascals like Faure, the notary, and many others who boasted that they had never read the abominable Civil Code promulgated under the Revolution. My uncle had his revenge by going to bed with all of the many pretty women who made Grenoble one of the jolliest provincial towns in France. The celebrated Laclos, whom I met, when he was an artillery general, in the box of the general staff at the Scala, and to whom I paid my respects as the author of *Les Liaisons Dangereuses,* grew quite *sentimental* when he learned that I came from Grenoble.

When my uncle, therefore, heard that I was leaving Grenoble to go to the Polytechnic Institute in Paris in November 1799, he took me aside and tried to give me two louis. I refused to take them, which no doubt pleased him, for he kept two or three apartments in the town and was always very short of money. With this matter disposed of, he assumed a paternal air that moved me deeply, for he had beautiful eyes, even though he squinted a bit under the stress of emotion. He then said:

"My boy, you think you have brains. You have done so well in mathematics at school that you have grown insufferable. But all that is worthless. You will only make your way in the world with the help of women. Now you are ugly, but no one will hold that against you because your face has character. Your mistresses will leave you after a while, to be sure, and remember this, it's very easy to become a laughingstock at such a moment. After that, in the eyes of the other women in the town, a man is not good enough to be thrown to the dogs. Now I tell you that within twenty-four hours after one woman has deserted you, you must be sure to make a declaration to another; if you can't find anyone better, make a declaration to a chambermaid."

With this he embraced me, and I climbed into the Lyons mail coach. How happy I might have been if I had remembered the advice of this great tactician! How many triumphs I missed! How many humiliations I suffered! But still, if I had been such a clever dog, by now I would have been sick to death of women, and consequently of music and painting as well, like my two contemporaries, M. de la Rosière and M. Perrochin, who are cold and world-weary, in short, philosophers. Instead of which I have been fortunate enough to be gulled in all matters concerning women, now as at the age of twenty-five.

It is for this reason that I shall never be driven to shoot myself out of boredom and disgust. In the literary field I still see many things to do. I have enough projects ahead of me to keep me busy for ten lives. My greatest difficulty at this moment, in 1832, is to accustom myself not to be distracted by office drudgery, such as making out a draft for 20,000 francs on the paymaster of the Treasury in Paris.

CHAPTER XI

⟨ ⟩

I DO NOT REMEMBER WHO IT WAS WHO BROUGHT ME TO the house of M. de l'Etang.[1]

He had somehow got me to send him a copy of my book, *Histoire de la Peinture en Italie*, it seems to me, on the pretext that he would write a review of it for the *Lycée*, one of those ephemeral journals that made the *Edinburgh Review*, by contrast, so popular in Paris.

In England, the aristocracy despises letters. In Paris, on the other hand, literature has too much importance. It is impossible for Parisians to tell the truth about the works of other Frenchmen who live in Paris.

I made eight or ten mortal enemies by telling the editors of the *Globe* to their faces that the *Globe* had too Puritanical a tone, and was perhaps lacking in *wit*. I meant this simply as a piece of friendly advice.

A literary magazine as conscientious as the *Edinburgh Review* was at that time would be out of the question in France, unless it were published in Geneva. The editor would have to be a businesslike fellow, capable of keeping a secret; he would make one trip a year to Paris, and would have the material for each issue sent to him in Geneva. He would select the articles, pay authors well (200 francs per page) and never reveal the names of his assistant editors.

One Sunday at two o'clock, at any rate, I was brought to meet M. de l'Etang, for it was at this inconvenient hour that he received his friends. You had to climb ninety-five steps to reach his apartment, since he kept his academy on the seventh floor of a house on the rue Gaillon that belonged to him and his sisters. His small windows looked out over a forest of chimney-pots, to me one of the ugliest sights in the world. But the four small rooms occupied by M. de l'Etang were charmingly decorated with engravings and curious art objects.

He owned a superb portrait of Cardinal Richelieu that I studied with interest, and a portrait of Racine, with his silly face, so heavy and fat. It was before he grew so fat that the great poet had experienced those emotions without which he could never have written *Andromaque* and *Phèdre*.

At M. de l'Etang's I found eight or ten persons gathered around a wretched little fire (for as I remember it was in February 1822 that I first came there) talking about everything under the sun. I was struck by the wit and good sense of the company, and particularly by the great tact of the master of the house, who, without seeming to obtrude, directed the discussion with such grace that there were never three people speaking at the same time, nor, for that matter, any uncomfortable pauses in the conversation.

I can scarcely say too much in praise of this circle. I have never found anything to equal it, certainly nothing that transcended it. The very first time I came there I was struck with admiration, and twenty times or more during the three or four years that the group came together, I found myself obliged to pay the same tribute.

Such a circle is possible only in the country of Voltaire, Molière, and Courier.[2]

It would be impossible to find the equivalent in England, for at M. de l'Etang's house they would have mocked at a duke as much as at anyone else, and perhaps more than at anyone else, if he were ridiculous.

Neither could Germany produce such a circle, for the Germans are too accustomed to accept the latest fashion in philosophical nonsense with the greatest enthusiasm (like M. Ancillon's Angels). Besides, apart from their enthusiasm, the Germans are too stupid.

Italians would have discoursed at length; each man would have held the floor for twenty minutes at a time and would have remained the mortal enemy of his opponent in the argument. At the third meeting they would have written satirical sonnets denouncing one another.

But here the discussion of all subjects was frank and sustained, with everyone taking part. Under the influence of M. de l'Etang, everyone was polite. He often found it necessary, however, to cover the retreat of some foolhardy guest who in his eager quest of some novel idea had gone too far afield and made himself absurd.

Among those I found there were M. Albert Stapfer, J. J. Ampère, Sautelet, and Lussinge.

M. de l'Etang is a character of the type of the good Vicar of Wakefield. To describe him adequately one would need to use all the delicate shading of Goldsmith or Addison.

To begin with, he is very ugly; one notices in particular his low, vulgar forehead, so rarely encountered in Paris. But he is well built and fairly tall.

He has all the pettiness of a bourgeois. If he buys a dozen handkerchiefs from the shopkeeper on the corner for thirty-six francs, two hours later he believes that he has made a rare find, and that you could not find anything in Paris to match those handkerchiefs at any price.

Notes

Introduction

1. Stendhal did not know that he was being read with great enjoyment during his own lifetime by the aged Goethe. Truly he was the "writer's writer." Balzac was unable to win readers for the *Chartreuse de Parme* by his exuberant praises. Nietzsche was, in part, inspired by him in his attempt at the "transvaluation" of moral values; while Tolstoy and Henry James (in the 1870s) esteemed him, although with moral reservations. Up to the 1880s at least, Stendhal seemed to appeal only to a choice few of the most masterly practitioners of his craft.

2. The equivalents of the code words, deciphered, are given in the text.

Chapter I

1. Stendhal, born in 1783, could scarcely have known Mme. Roland—"Oh Liberty, what crimes are committed in thy name!"—one of the Girondin leaders, guillotined during the Terror of 1793. Gabriel Gros was his instructor at the Ecole Centrale of Grenoble, and also an active local champion of the Republic.

2. Count Jacques-Claude Beugnot, socially prominent during the First Empire, turned to the Bourbon party before Waterloo.

3. "Countess Dulong" was Clémentine (daughter of the Count and Countess Beugnot), who later married Count de Curial. Her mother, Countess Beugnot, had been in earlier years the mistress of one of Beyle's friends—always the kind hostess and wise counselor to Beyle also.

4. Metilda Viscontini Dembowska, of an old Milanese family, was married to General Jan Dembowski of Napoleon's army in Italy, from whom she was later separated. She was the friend of the patriot-poet Ugo Foscolo; in 1821, suspected by the Austrian police of being implicated in the Carbonari conspiracies, she was put through a long and cruel examination, out of which she emerged without exposing her friends.

5. Henry Martineau, the great French Stendhal scholar, sees this as a free transcription of one of Shelley's posthumous poems beginning: "The sighs I breathe . . ." But since Beyle's quotations are always from memory, and nearly always inexact, it might also have echoed the better-known *Ode to the Night*: "I sighed for thee . . .".

6. The Baroness Traversi was a cousin of Metilda, a woman of wealth, who disliked Beyle and tried to prejudice Metilda against him.

7. Mlle. Sophie Duvaucel, later Mme. de Villeneuve, a woman of great intelligence and considerable erudition, a close friend of Mérimée, Sutton-Sharpe and Beyle.

8. On June 3, 1819, Beyle had followed Metilda from Milan to the town of Volterra, where she had gone to see her son at school. Since she had expressly forbidden him to do so, she was extremely annoyed when he turned up, disguised in smoked glasses.

9. These cryptic symbols in the manuscript, discovered by the scholar Louis Royer, are generally interpreted to mean "tuer Louis XVIII," i.e., "kill Louis XVIII." In other words, since his life was worthless to him, Beyle planned to sacrifice it by assassinating the king.

Chapter II

1. "Lussinge" was the Baron Adolph de Mareste, a friend of many literary notables of the 1820s and 1830s, and much esteemed by them. The "dreadful misfortune" of September 15, 1826 was Beyle's break with his mistress, Clémentine de Curial. The *Roman Comique* was a well-known "burlesque" by Scarron.
2. The Countess d'Argout. The Count d'Argout had been one of Beyle's comrades as auditor at the court of Napoleon; later he became a cabinet minister under the Bourbons.
3. Stendhal himself was under five foot five.
4. At the prefecture of police.
5. Maisonnette was Joseph Lingay, a political journalist and ghost-writer for various Ministers of the ultra-Royalist party before 1830; afterwards for anti-Royalists as well.
6. This was Albert de Rubempré, who lived on the rue Bleu—hence the alias "Mme. Azur." The daughter of a theatrical producer, she was something of an eccentric bluestocking, always wore black robes, kept the windows of her apartment curtained day and night, and took up spiritism for a time. In 1828 she became Beyle's mistress for a few months.
7. Nicolas-Rémy Lolot, an industrialist, not a banker, who owned two nail factories and had a part interest in a glass factory.
8. Nothing more is known of this apparently close friend of Beyle.
9. Considered by modern scholars to be Mme. Victor de Tracy.
10. Martineau thinks that this must have been Mme. d'Argout, the wife of Beyle's associate in the Council of State under Napoleon, not Mme. Daru, whom he courted for many years, but who died in 1815.
11. The true Barot, a notable lawyer and later prime minister for a short period in 1847–48, not the false Barot mentioned earlier, whose name was really Lolot.
12. The Countess Beugnot, mother of Clémentine de Curial. After

mentioning Mme. Beugnot by her real name in the preceding
chapter, Beyle now disguises it as "Doligny."

13. A Napoleonic title, legally extinguished in 1815. This was the
younger brother of Count Pierre Daru, Napoleon's Quartermaster-
General, and a distant cousin of Beyle. It was through the influence
of the Darus that Beyle found a career in the service of Napoleon.

14. At Daru's request, when he was about to be married.

15. Louis Louvel, who assassinated the Duke of Berry in 1820. He
was tried and executed.

Chapter III

1. Thus in English in the text.

2. "In the simple costume of beauty just wrenched from sleep."
From Racine's *Britannicus*.

3. *Babillan*: one who is impotent, a eunuch, a word possibly of
Italian origin. Beyle here recalls Mme. Azur's testimony on his
behalf in 1829. This may have been verbal, but the letters of
Clémentine de Curial of earlier date, found among the Stendhal
papers, furnish written testimony of his claims to normality.

4. Of the Scala Theatre in Milan.

5. Count Saurau was governor of Lombardy, grand chancellor of
the Austrian Empire, etc.

Chapter IV

1. After he recovered somewhat from his rupture with Clémentine
de Curial.

2. As a matter of fact, M. de Tracy suffered from cataracts.

3. Jean-Louis Gros, adjutant-general of the Imperial Guard in
1813.

4. In Rome.

5. Favras was implicated in a plot to help Louis XVI escape from the
Châtelet late in 1789. His trial dragged on for two months, the

witnesses disagreeing, but an armed attempt of the Royalists on the prison on January 26, 1790, sealed his fate. He was hanged on February 19, 1790. The King's brother, later Louis XVIII, was one of the conspirators, and it was not known whether Favras would reveal his name or not before he was hanged. When word came at last that Favras had died without betraying his fellow-conspirators, the royal plotter, who in his anxiety had postponed his dinner several hours, turned to his entourage and said: "Let us go to the table."

6. Dangeau, a brave soldier, an inveterate gambler, and an intimate of Louis XIV, was a model of the perfect courtier.

7. An anecdote that was often repeated, although Ségur himself claimed merely that he had borrowed the pen of the British Ambassador.

8. This is one of the occasions when Beyle slips into his somewhat imperfect English.

9. Louis-Philippe.

10. The day when the Revolution of 1830 broke out, overthrowing Charles X and leading to the accession of Louis-Philippe, the "citizen king."

11. July 26, 1830, when the decrees suppressing the freedom of the press and annulling the recent elections were promulgated by the Bourbons.

12. Pierre-François Réal, a councilor of state under Napoleon. His daughter was rated heroic by Beyle because she helped her father escape from France in 1815 and then followed him to America.

Chapter V

1. "Making one's street" was a common form of real-estate development at that period; the owner of a piece of property in a growing city cut through his land and lined it with houses, the street thus created usually bearing his name.

2. This reference and the one to lemons, above, are incomplete in the text. Both concern some youthful gallantries or escapades of M. de Tracy. The anecdote about his lieutenant-colonel dates back to the period of the Constituent Assembly, when Tracy, on learning that the regiment he commanded was about to emigrate, rode with all speed to the border, and delivering a short patriotic speech, saved his men from going over to the enemies of France.

3. Beyle is referring here to the fact that Levasseur supplanted him as consul at Trieste in 1830. But although Levasseur won the post through Lafayette's influence, Beyle lost it for another reason, because he was persona non grata to the Austrian police.

4. A liberal newspaper of the Restoration period, suppressed by the Bourbons.

5. Victor Jacquemont, who wrote a series of admirable travel letters, died a short time after writing Beyle, while exploring the high Himalayas.

6. The reference is to an apocryphal anecdote about Talleyrand's arranging a hunt for Napoleon. Since the Foreign Minister had no game in his park at Auteuil, he ordered some 5,000 tame rabbits at the Paris market and let them loose on the grounds. Having been starved for a day the rabbits, instead of fleeing before the hunters, ran up to them, and Napoleon is said to have killed a large number before he realized that it was all a trick. The tale goes on to the effect that Talleyrand let loose a big black pig from his own barnyard in the Bois de Boulogne so that Napoleon could have the pleasure of hunting "big game."

7. Mme. de Laubépin, a daughter of the elder Tracys, mentioned later by Stendhal under her right name.

8. A compendium or pocket encyclopedia of historical and current events, considered quite an achievement in its time.

9. Martineau believes that "Céline" was Mme. Victor de Tracy, elsewhere referred to by Beyle as the Marquise de Rosine, and under her own name as well. She was probably much in his thoughts

at the time of his writing this memoir, because she had used her influence in liberal circles to win him his appointment as consul after the Revolution of 1830.

10. Magendie was a distinguished physiologist of the time; Baron Gérard was a prosperous portrait painter, whose salon Beyle visited every Wednesday during his stay in Paris; Saint-Jean d'Angely was a member of Napoleon's Council of State, a powerful figure in the First Empire.

11. He had had some sharp words with Thierry, the lion of her salon.

12. Romain Colomb, a native of Grenoble and Beyle's first cousin, was his literary executor, who after his death made valiant efforts to have his works reprinted, and saw to it that all his posthumous writings were carefully preserved.

13. Louis Crozet, native of Grenoble, was Beyle's most intimate friend in his youth.

14. Boulevard des Italians.

15. Louis de Barral, a member of a noble family of Grenoble.

16. Mlle. Angelina Bereyter or Bereiter, a native of Strasbourg, whose tenderness and complaisance could not make Beyle forget his unsatisfied passion for the Countess Daru.

17. "Not at all," a polite contradiction.

Chapter VI

1. In later life Beyle discontinued keeping a journal; but with the recovery of many volumes of his library a quantity of autobiographical notes were found, and precise dates as well, shedding light on his opinions, friendships and love affairs.

2. He seems to have forgotten what he wrote in Chapter I, namely that he went on this trip with money that he had entrusted to M. Petit at the Hotel de Bruxelles. Or, as he admits later, he may have confused certain details with those of a later trip, made in 1826, or an earlier one, made in 1817.

3. Henry Beyle, Milanese, lived, wrote, loved; this soul adored Cimarosa, Mozart and Shakespeare. Died at the age of . . . , the . . . 18 . . .
4. The city of his birth.
5. "There you will repair to the cool shade." Incorrectly quoted from Virgil's *Bucolics*.
6. Domenico Fiore, a Naples lawyer. The *Jupiter Mansuetus* was a statue that Napoleon brought back from Italy along with the rest of his fabulous loot in paintings and sculpture. It was on view at the Louvre until the fall of the Empire when it was returned to the Vatican.
7. Smith or Schmit, sometimes mentioned in Beyle's correspondence as a Belgian who had something to do with gaining an entree to English magazines and publishers for his writings.
8. Prefect of Police and later Prime Minister under the Bourbons.
9. By Bernardin de Saint-Pierre.
10. An old friend of Beyle's in the French Foreign Office, under the Bourbons, who sent him to Rome on a secret mission in 1829.
11. One of the highest decorations awarded by the Kings of France, the chevalier de Saint-Esprit.
12. A comedy by N. Lemercier, in which Talma appeared in the leading role. It was a thinly veiled attack on "usurpers" and therefore displeasing to Napoleon.
13. The Baron Francisque de Syon, although hailed as a young man of brilliant promise, did not in fact accomplish much during his lifetime. Among his few published works is one that appeared in the middle of the century, attacking the parliamentary system, modern journalism and literature, and Pope Pius IX, as a dangerous liberal. This change of face would have amused Beyle enormously had he lived to witness it. The Duchess of Trémoille's salon was the meeting-place of the ultra-Royalists.
14. In English, sic.
15. Sic—Beyle's idea of how the word was spelled in English.

16. Barot (Lolot) was part owner of a crystal factory known as Vonèche-Baccarat. The reference to carding machines may indicate that he had some textile interests as well.

17. Stendhal here uses a word of his own invention: "absurbe," which speaks for itself.

18. In English, sic.

Chapter VII

1. And my verse, good or bad, always has something to say.

2. A noble poverty is all that remains to me.

3. Mélanie Guilbert, Beyle's first mistress, whom he met in Paris when he was twenty years of age, and for whose sake he went to Marseilles to go into business. Séraphie T. was a Mme. Tivollier, a friend of the Beyle family, to whom he paid court while living with Mélanie.

4. According to Professor Trompeo, the Italian Stendhal scholar, this might have been the Marchesa Potengiani, whose first name was Angelica, and whose acquaintance Beyle had recently made in Rome.

5. Pierre-Jean de Béranger, poet and songwriter, whose lyrics, much admired by Beyle, enjoyed nationwide popularity.

6. A play "in imitation of" or adapted from Shakespeare, Shakespeare being considered at that time too coarse for literal translation.

7. Talma and Mme. de Staël? Or Talma and the stilted alexandrine of the French classical drama, overthrown by the Romantic revolution of 1830?

8. Incomplete sentence in the text. Many scholars believe that the word "ti . . ." was intended as "tyranny," always ripe for a fall according to Beyle.

9. William Sutton-Sharp, an English lawyer of long residence in Paris, a close friend of Beyle, Mérimée and other men of letters.

Chapter VIII

1. Joseph Lingay.
2. These three men, in turn, headed the Ministry of Police or the Interior during the 1820s.
3. Beyle himself.
4. The offices of the *Journal des Débats*.
5. Charles-Guillaume Etienne, who was editor-in-chief of several of the most important literary reviews of the time, and Victor-Joseph Etienne, later known as de Jouy.
6. *La Minerve Française*, a liberal review to which Jouy contributed.
7. Cotin was a seventeenth-century poet satirized by Boileau and others.
8. Where does the oak leaf go?
   —I go where the wind does blow.
9. At the court of Napoleon.
10. Mme. N. C. D. is the Countess Daru; Cideville is Bècheville, near Meulan, her country seat, where Stendhal visited her frequently around 1811.
11. Béranger.

Chapter IX

1. French scholars have discovered that the lady's name was *Chanson*, for which Beyle substituted *Romance*, both words having the same meaning in French.
2. Cours de Gebelin was a scholar of the eighteenth century who made some early studies in primitive society and language.
3. As mentioned in the introduction, Count Gazul was Prosper Mérimée.
4. Claude-Joseph Dorat, a poet and playwright of the eighteenth century, an imitator of Voltaire, prolific and boring.

5. The scholar-detectives have not been able to trace the identity of this young woman.

6. Beyle was only slightly acquainted with Mme. Guizot and Mme. Récamier. He is not known to have frequented any of the salons here mentioned, although he corresponded with the husband of Mme. de Broglie, and wrote articles about the works of Mme. de Duras, who was the author of several popular novels.

7. The Countess Saint-Aulaire, wife of the French ambassador to Rome at this time.

8. Samuel Rogers, poet-laureate and uncle of Beyle's friend Sutton-Sharpe.

9. Sic, in English in the text.

10. This refers perhaps to Beyle's escapade of 1819, when he followed Metilda to Volterra in disguise, mentioned earlier in these memoirs.

11. One can only suppose that Beyle read more hypocrisy into Byron's letter of May 29, 1823 than the known character of the poet would justify. In this communication Byron thanks the author of *Rome, Naples et Florence*, for "a very flattering mention," and then goes on to take issue with him in his analysis of Scott's character: "I have known Walter Scott long and well . . . and I can assure you that his character is worthy of admiration—that of all men he is the most *open*, the most *amiable* . . . I say that Walter Scott is as nearly a thorough good man as can be, because I *know* it by experience to be the case."

12. The book sold seventeen copies in ten years.

13. On his consular uniform.

14. Countess Clémentine de Curial, a Royalist, sometimes quarreled with Beyle over his political views.

Chapter X

1. Another pseudonym for Clémentine de Curial, the daughter of Mme. Beugnot, disguised again below as the Marquise de N. . . .

Chapter XI

1. Etienne Delécluze, the foremost art critic of the day.
2. Paul Louis Courier, former artillery officer, later a vigorous and courageous pamphleteer, one of the few contemporaries Beyle admired and ranked with Voltaire.